underlined

Transcendence with
the Human Body in Art

DOUG ADAMS

Transcendence with the Human Body in Art

George Segal, Stephen De Staebler, Jasper Johns, and Christo

CROSSROAD • NEW YORK

1991
The Crossroad Publishing Company
370 Lexington Avenue, New York, NY 10017

Copyright 1991 by Doug Adams

The work of Jasper Johns is © Jasper Johns/VAGA, New York 1991.
The work of Piet Mondrian is © Piet Mondrian/VAGA, New York 1991.
The work of George Segal is © George Segal/VAGA, New York 1991.

Library of Congress Cataloging-in-Publication Data

Adams, Doug.
  Transcendence with the human body in art : Segal, De Staebler,
Johns, and Christo / by Doug Adams.
    p. cm.
  Includes bibliographical references.
  ISBN 0-8245-1104-2 (cloth)
  1. Art and religion—United States.   2. Art, Modern—20th century-
-United States.   3. Figurative art—United States.   4. Transcendence
(Philosophy) I. Title.
N6512.5.F5A34   1991
701'.04—dc20   91-17700
                                                         CIP

Contents

Preface

Human bodies and biblical subject matter appear with increasing frequency in contemporary American art. In this book, I explore theological perceptions of such art where transcendence is expressed and experienced with the human body. While these artworks express awareness of our bodily finitude, they model experiences of our capacities to make connections with others beyond ourselves and sometimes with God as center. Insights of the art differ decisively from insights of postmodern a/theology developed by Mark Taylor. In the art, we discern shapes for postmodern theologies with a sense of place and time.

George Segal's *The Holocaust* and other works reflect biblical subject matter and God as center. Stephen De Staebler's sculptures relate to religious forms and times of graceful aging, dying, and rising. Jasper Johns's paintings parallel postcritical philosophies overcoming subject/object and mind/body dichotomies. Christo's *The Running Fence* and other process and land art embrace wider communities and the earth. The method of art historian Joshua Taylor and the epistemologies of philosophers Michael Polanyi and Ludwig Wittgenstein further illumine transcendence in the experience of contemporary American art. First and

foremost throughout this book, look at the art. As Wittgenstein advised in relation to verbal structures, "Don't think;
look!" Linking the titles of two Joshua Taylor books, readers
discern that by "learning to look" one recognizes that "to
see is to think."

I thank many persons who have aided in the development of this book. Artists George Segal, Stephen De
Staebler, Alice Lok Cahana, Christo, and Jeanne-Claude
Christo gave generously of their time, carefully reading the
drafts of these chapters and granting interviews that deep-
ened my insights. The president of Rice University, George
Rupp, and its Department of Religious Studies chairper-
son, Niels Nielsen, evoked the nucleus of this book by their
invitation to deliver the Rockwell Lectures in Houston,
Texas. Jane Blaffer Owen immensely aided my analysis of
De Staebler's art through her support of my studies of his
works in New Harmony, her commission of his *Pietà* (after
the second Rockwell Lecture outlined how important such
a work could be in advancing the relation of visual arts and
religion), and a grant from the Sarah Campbell Blaffer
Foundation for the subvention of the illustrations in this
book.

Jane Dillenberger, John Dillenberger, and Diane Apostolos-Cappadona read and reread this manuscript prompt-
ing valuable editorial revisions. James O. Duke aided my
understanding of postmodern a/theology; and Jerry H. Gill
located many of Wittgenstein's quotations to develop chapter 3. At Pacific School of Religion, faculty secretaries
Audrey Englert and Barbara Anderson carefully and cheerfully attended to numerous details in processing the manuscript.

With this book, Werner Mark Linz and Frank Oveis of

Crossroad Publishing Company continue a long record of supporting scholarship relating art and religion. Besides her editorial suggestions, Diane Apostolos-Cappadona aided this book by arranging for many permissions and photographs so indispensable for readers to experience transcendence with the human body.

George Segal's *The Holocaust*: Biblical Subject Matter and God as Center

*P*erceptions of transcendence and biblical subject matter appear in many sculptures by
contemporary artist George Segal (b. 1924). An in-depth
examination of Segal's most extensive sculpture, *The Holocaust*, reveals how art not only meaningfully relates our
twentieth-century world to biblical studies and historical
theology but also encourages multiple interpretations and
interfaith appreciation. Segal's postmodern art differs decisively from the insights Mark Taylor and other death of
God theologians have developed as their postmodern a/
theology. In Segal's work, relationships with a center beyond self are suggestive for postmodern theologies yet to be
rendered in verbal forms.

As a postmodern artist, Segal affirms historic subject
matter and transcendence through the human body. In
contrast, modern artists tended toward abstraction that
eliminated the overt human form along with recognizable
subject matter in the art of the 1940s and 1950s. Modern
American artists such as Barnett Newman (1905–70) and
Mark Rothko (1903–70) had advocated abstraction as the

way to express and experience the transcendent; but George Segal asserts that transcendence comes through explicit articulation of the human body in art.[1] George Segal's *The Holocaust* (1984: The Legion of Honor Museum, San Francisco) (fig. 1) unites the twentieth-century Holocaust with subjects from the Hebrew and Christian scriptures. Transcendence of one's own time and place occurs as the art work stretches thoughts into the biblical milieu. Transcendence is modeled by the sculpture's figures who relate with a center beyond themselves and reach out to touch others.

The placement of *The Holocaust* increases the possibilities for ambiguity of interpretation and transcendence of any one viewpoint by inviting the viewer to make choices as to approach and to angle of vision (and to realize there are other approaches one could take). Some proposals (one by Lawrence Halprin) would have placed the work conspicuously in the center of the Legion of Honor's front parking lot replacing a large fountain. Finally, the sculpture was placed to the north below the parking lot and behind a chest high wall. Thus visitors may walk from the parking lot toward the museum without seeing *The Holocaust*. Allowing each person to avoid seeing Segal's sculpture is appropriate in a time when some try to deny that the actual Holocaust occurred.

In this instance, the artist is responsible for the placement of the sculpture. Segal noted, "I don't want to inflict it. I mentally cringed at the idea of having to place that sculpture in that central fountain."[2] Asked if he intended to present the work to encourage multiple approaches and interpretations, he responded affirmatively.

1. George Segal, *The Holocaust*, 1984. White bronze, wood, and wire. 10×10×20 feet Legion of Honor Museum, San Francisco. Photograph by Doug Adams. © George Segal/VAGA, New York 1991.

Yes. I gave that idea to the landscape architect. I
designed the conception of that space. It was
executed according to my ideas. I was the one
who requested it. There was a terrible tangle of
bushes; and they thought I was crazy. I wanted it
private. It's one of the most extraordinary views in
the world. It's a spectacular piece of nature. I
wanted essentially private and individual responses. I didn't want a big public ringing of a
gong.[3]

An examination of the sculpture and Segal's comments
clarify how the work's multiple perspectives, which require
choices by the individual viewer, are paradigmatic of differences between postmodern art and premodern art.

In approaching the sculpture from the parking lot, one
views it from above (fig. 1). While one stands above the
sculpture, the nearest figures are a fullbodied young couple
to the right and the figure of a heavyset man and boy to the
left. One has a choice of turning away or going down into
the sculpture by one of two routes (a stairway to the left or a
ramp to the right). These routes lead the viewer to enter
into the sculpture from opposite sides. From the foot of the
steps at the left is a pile of four emaciated bodies reminiscent of the thousand concentration camp photographs
which Segal studied. From the foot of the ramp at the right,
a Venus-like young woman lies perpendicular to an Adonis-
like young man as her head rests on his right side (fig. 2).

Her head rests on his right rib cage. She holds a partially
eaten apple in her left hand. While she senses no one other
than the young man in the sculpture, his left arm rests on
the abdomen of the central figure. So the young man could

2. Detail of Segal, *The Holocaust*. Photograph by Doug Adams. ©
George Segal/VAGA, New York 1991.

3. Detail of Segal, *The Holocaust*. Photograph by Doug Adams. ©
George Segal/VAGA, New York 1991.

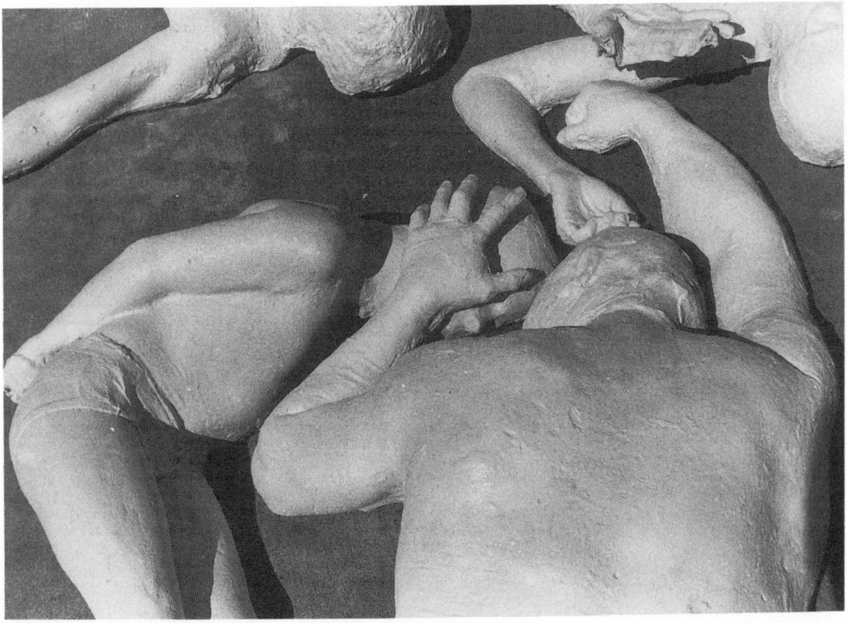

be aware of the central figure's breathing, although he could see only that central figure's right hand which supports or shapes his own right hand. The young man and woman are clothed only around their loins.

With biblical awareness, one may identify these figures as Adam and Eve and God. God formed Adam who was animated by God's breath (Gen. 2:7). Eve was formed from the rib taken out of Adam's side (Gen. 2:21–22) and was the first to eat the forbidden fruit (Gen. 3:6). After eating the fruit, Adam and Eve put on loincloths (Gen. 3:7) and no longer wished to see God face to face (Gen. 3:8–10). So one confronts the question of the relation of Adam and Eve to *The Holocaust* and sees the central figure as God.

To the left of the central figure is another configuration. The older man and the young boy see only each other (fig. 3). The boy's vision of the older man's action is obscured by the latter's left hand placed over the right side of the former's face. The boy's hands are tightly drawn up behind his back as if bound. At first, the man seems to be protecting the boy or shielding him from seeing anything troubling. However, closer scrutiny reveals that his right hand is a fist separated from the boy's head only by the central figure's intervening left arm. While the raised fist could be protesting the boy's condition, it might also be about to smash the boy's head. If one were to remove the central figure's intervening hand, the father's fist would appear a threat to the boy. Then the father's left hand would appear to be holding the boy's head down so he cannot see what the father's right hand is about to do.

Biblical insights suggest the identification of the boy as Isaac, the man as Abraham about to sacrifice his son, and the central figure as God's intervening angel. Abraham

bound Isaac to sacrifice him; but the angel of God inter-
vened to prevent Abraham from raising his hand against
Isaac (Gen. 22:9–12).

Segal had twice before created sculptures with the theme
of Abraham nearly sacrificing Isaac. His presentation of this
theme in *The Holocaust* differs significantly from the earlier
versions although it resonates with some of their dynamics.
The Sacrifice of Isaac (1973: Tel Aviv Museum, Tel Aviv)
(fig. 4) presents a man and a boy near the ages of those in
The Holocaust, but the man stands with his arms down at
his sides. While his right hand holds a knife, it is pointed
back away from the boy. His left hand is clenched more in
tension than threat. He appears to resist sacrificing his son.
In that sculpture, Isaac is on the ground but facing upward.
A raised shoulder, a bent knee, and a face looking toward
his father give the impression he is about to rise not to
escape but to relate physically with his father.

Such an understanding of the 1973 sculpture corresponds
to a positive interpretation of Abraham's gestures toward
Isaac in *The Holocaust*. Both works affirm the figures' continuing relation to the earth. In *The Sacrifice of Isaac*, the
boy is positioned on a large rock as the altar of sacrifice.
Segal stated that "in Israel the people and the rock felt to
me one material."[4] In *The Holocaust*, Abraham lies down
with Isaac; and so, they become nearly one. The curving
shapes of the figures on the ground resonate with the
surrounding landscape. *The Sacrifice of Isaac* was unveiled
in Tel Aviv a few months before the Yom Kippur war. Segal
responded to a comment that his work was too prophetic by
saying, "Abraham did not kill Isaac; all of us are working
precisely for that."[5]

Another Segal sculptural treatment of the sacrifice of

4. George Segal, *The Sacrifice of Isaac*, 1973. White plaster. 7 × 9 × 8½
feet. The Mann Auditorium, Tel Aviv, Israel. Photograph by Ron Erde.
© George Segal/VAGA, New York 1991.

Isaac corresponds to a less benign understanding of Abraham's gestures toward his son in *The Holocaust*. *In Memory of May 4, 1970, Kent State: Abraham and Isaac* (1978: Princeton University, Princeton) (fig. 5) was commissioned by Kent State University as a memorial to the four students killed by national guardsmen in 1970 during an antiwar protest. The father stands with his right hand holding a knife pointed at the chest of the kneeling son who is of college age. Viewed from the side, the knife's shape and position, protruding at the father's groin level, may be interpreted as a phallic symbol. The son looks up to the father. However, if the son should stand, he would tower over the father. The son is a person of greater physical stature than the father. The young man's hands are bound before him. He does not raise them but lowers them; so, he does not appear either to threaten his father or to protect himself. The father appears ignoble and the son noble in that rendering. Kent State rejected the sculpture which has since been located outside the chapel at Princeton University.[6]

The presentation of Abraham in *The Holocaust* is ambiguous allowing for interpretations from either of those two earlier sculptures. Two additional Segal sculptures deal with biblical texts associated with the Abraham cycle and the theme of separation that culminates in the sacrifice of Isaac. In *Abraham's Farewell to Ishmael* (1987: Private Collection) (fig. 6), all four figures are standing. Three of them are positioned in front of a huge rock reminiscent of Segal's previous use of a rock as the altar of sacrifice. Sarah stands slightly behind the rock viewing the other three or presiding over this event. In the biblical story, she had insisted

5. George Segal, *In Memory of May 4, 1979: Abraham and Isaac*, Kent State University 1979. Bronze. $81 \times 60 \times 112$ inches. The John B. Putnam Collection, Princeton University. © George Segal/VAGA, New York 1991.

that Abraham send Ishmael away with his mother Hagar. Hagar as Sarah's servant had served as a surrogate mother to produce an heir for Abraham; but later, Sarah herself produced Isaac and wanted Abraham to eliminate Ishmael and Hagar so they would present no threat to Isaac's inheritance (Gen. 21:9–10). Sarah's effort to separate Abraham and Hagar was evident in the original installation of the sculpture as it was positioned so that viewers came through the gallery door and approached it from an angle to the left of that shown in the photograph. From that angle, the viewers saw Sarah between Hagar to their right and Abraham embracing Ishmael to their left. In the wilderness, Hagar feared her son would die, but the angel of God intervenes so Ishmael lives (Gen. 21:17–21). That story is seen as prefiguring the sacrifice of Isaac in the next chapter of Genesis where the angel of God intervenes to spare his life.[7]

In the sculpture, Abraham embraces Ishmael while Hagar stands in the foreground with her arms around her own body. Her arms echo the positions of Abraham's arms around Ishmael. Each right forearm is diagonally positioned with the hand embracing a left shoulder: Abraham's hand embraces Ishmael's shoulder while Hagar's hand embraces her own shoulder. Abraham's and Hagar's left forearms are parallel to the ground with fingers spread in an open position to embrace a side: Abraham's hand embraces Ishmael's side and Hagar's hand embraces her own side.

A much earlier sculpture dealt with another text of separation which is associated with the Abraham cycle even though Abraham is not portrayed in the work. *The Legend of Lot* (1966: Sidney Janis Gallery, New York) places together two separate episodes. The standing figure of Lot's

6. George Segal, *Abraham's Farewell to Ishmael*, 1987. Painted plaster. 102×78 ×78 inches. Sidney Janis Gallery, New York. © George Segal/ VAGA, New York 1991.

wife turns into a pillar of salt as she turns back to Sodom and Gomorrah (and away from a scene of the second later episode which depicts incest between his daughters and Lot). The unconscious Lot lies beneath one daughter who mounts him while a second daughter stands nearby observing the scene and awaiting her turn.

Those two stories parody two Abraham stories. The first story involves Lot's wife leaving a city but unfaithfully turning back (Gen. 19:26) in contrast to Abraham and Sarah faithfully going forth from Ur and not turning back (Gen. 12). The second story deals with the problem of continuing the family line by recourse to someone other than one's legal wife. In the Lot story, the surrogates are his daughters as they make Lot drunk and lie with him in violation of Jewish law (Gen. 19:31–38). In contrast, Sarah's servant Hagar serves as the surrogate with Abraham in conformity with the customs of the day. Thus both faithfulness and unfaithfulness are included in those biblical stories.

Segal intends that the viewer remember the full biblical tradition that includes the Abraham cycle and the creation story in *The Holocaust*.[8] How are we to understand these familiar biblical subjects in this new configuration titled *The Holocaust*? There are several possibilities. First, the word holocaust is associated with the word sacrifice in the Hebrew scriptures. This holocaust may be interpreted through the story of sacrifice as presented in the story of Abraham and Isaac or through the story of Adam and Eve. In these instances, the central figure is an angel of God or God.

However, there is more to be seen. The central figure and one of those in the heap are in cruciform positions (fig. 1). The body at the right foot of the central figure resembles similar positions of those at the foot or leg of Jesus in traditional depictions of the crucifixion and deposition (fig. 7). The implicit or explicit presentation of a Christological interpretation arises which is, of course, problematic if the Jewish artist did not intend it as a possibility. In considering such an interpretation of the central figure as a cruciform, particularly when approached through the body at that figure's foot, Segal responded affirmatively.

> I think it is very valid. Absolutely. The cruciform, I was thinking of the cruciform; but I haven't spoken about that in public. [9]

The central figure becomes Christ from one viewpoint but becomes God or God's angel from other viewpoints. Segal cited Søren Kierkegaard's *Fear and Trembling* as a model for his own use of multiple approaches and interpretations:

> One of my favorite books on this whole subject was Kierkegaard's *Fear and Trembling*: five astoundingly different movie scenarios, Kierkegaard's private idea of five different lines of feverish thought going through Abraham's head on the way to Moriah. That has been for me a valuable trigger. [10]

Segal was referring to the "Exordium" section in *Fear and Trembling* where there are four such "scenarios" which in combination with the biblical account (which Kierkegaard explored in the "Eulogy on Abraham" immediately after the "Exordium") make five. [11]

an emaciated woman in the heap. Both women add affirmations of life. Eve's genital area is prominent; she appears more living than dead (fig. 2). Her sensuality contributes to the sense of lively survival as Segal acknowledged. Eve suggests abundance of nature, a regenerative image. Segal stated, "I became as interested in Eve's sensuality as anything else. . . . It has to do with survival."[14]

The nakedness of the emaciated woman resonates with the nakedness of the central figure as a comparison of their two torsos shows (fig. 7 and 9). Segal explained how the historic Holocaust influenced his inclusion of only two women:

> In all the research I did, the men and women were mostly segregated. I started doing only males and then I decided even though they literally didn't die together, they did. I decided I had to add women. The whole thing just grew. I steeped myself in all the information; and then I just went on gut reaction.[15]

Although that second woman could be seen as in rigor mortis, her hands held aloft in an upright position suggest postures of biblical prayer, blessing, or benediction. Segal remarked,

> The woman who posed is a dancer who invents her own choreography; and we had been talking about rigor mortis. I think she added that herself—the supplication, something like the gesture used in blessing the sabbath candle.[16]

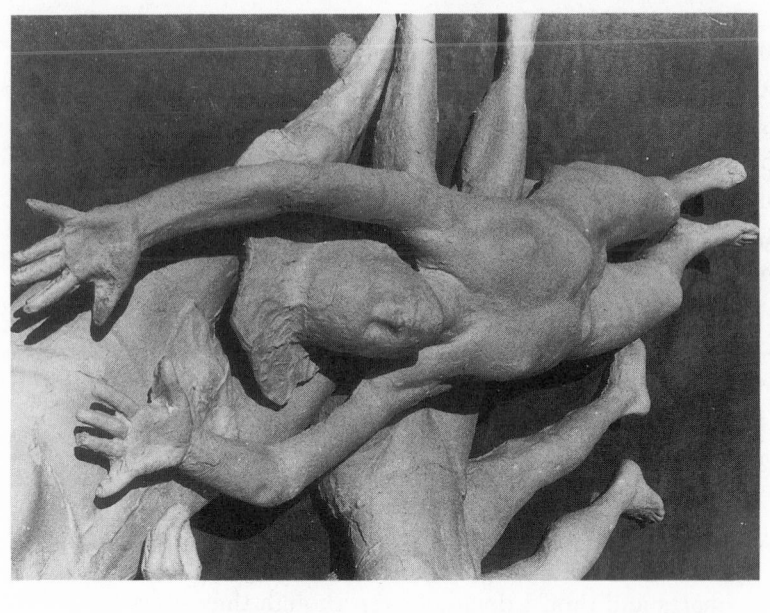

9. Detail of Segal, *The Holocaust*. Photograph by Doug Adams. © George Segal/VAGA, New York 1991.

8. Detail of Segal, *The Holocaust*. Photograph by Doug Adams. © George Segal/VAGA, New York 1991.

The hair of the woman resembles the iconography of Lilith who according to Jewish tradition was Adam's first wife. Created co-equal with Adam, she was later seen in art and dance as causing chaos.[17] As the most hellish scene in the sculpture, the pile of bodies is most appropriately placed to the central figure's lower left; for traditionally, hell is to Christ's lower left in last judgment paintings and sculptures while the blessed are placed to Christ's right.

There are ten figures on the ground which might signify the ten persons required for a *minyan* or quorum in Jewish worship. Segal reported,

> I built the sculpture one figure at a time. . . . I just kept going; and it kept growing until it seemed enough. I wasn't consciously thinking about a *minyan*. The sculpture stopped when it seemed complete.[18]

The person standing at the barb wire fence with his back to all the others appears lonely and more dead than alive (fig. 8). Segal intended to maintain an ambiguity about this figure's attitude by keeping his hand a little distance above the wire. Some visitors push the wire down under the standing figure's hand. In the original conception, Segal had planned to have the man's hand touch a wire as he had in the maquette, the sculpture's original plaster model now at the Jewish Museum in New York; but not wanting suicide to be suggested by the gesture of a hand touching wires that were electrified in camps, Segal kept a short distance between that hand and the wire in the final installation. This is the only isolated figure in the sculpture. All the rest touch or are touched by at least one other person.

In comparison with his isolation, the figures on the ground appear more interactive. Their interrelation defies the horror of Holocaust. On the ground, all of the figures' heads point inward toward the central figure and so establish a strong sense of relationship that would diminish if all the bodies were to be turned around in the opposite direction with their heads far away from the central figure. (The sense of exposure and vulnerability would increase in that reversed position where the heads would be exposed to the periphery instead of the present composition where their feet and hands come between the periphery and their heads.)

When they first come to *The Holocaust*, many visitors see only the horror of death or expect to see only that. However, once they look more closely at some of the figures, they see details and sense relationships that witness to life. Life or death may be seen. Multiple interpretations of *The Holocaust* are possible. One may begin with Abraham and Isaac or Adam and Eve. The Christian scriptures are evoked as well as the Hebrew scriptures. Furthermore, a cruciform or star of David may be seen in the overall composition. The central figure may be interpreted in many ways: as God, as God's angel, as Christ, or as an embodiment of nature. In these very choices and ambiguities, any one view or interpretation is transcended.

Experiences of transcendence are modeled through the relations of the different bodies in the sculpture; for each body senses only partially (usually without seeing) something beyond himself or herself. The viewer sees explicitly the larger context that each figure only partially senses tacitly. Some viewers walk by and perceive little beyond a jumble of bodies; but there is much to discover here that places Holocaust in a larger context of biblical and theological study. In an interview with the *Northern California Jewish Bulletin*,

> Segal said he wanted the content of the sculpture to go further than the symbolism of those who perished in the Holocaust. In addition, he says, he wanted "to talk about people from the Bible Adam and Eve; Abraham and Isaac and my intent is for people to discover them."[19]

In that discovery, both the Holocaust and the viewer become connected to times and places beyond oneself; and one feels not only death but life.

While willing to confirm his multiple original intentions including Adam and Eve, Abraham and Isaac, and the cruciform, Segal is most concerned that viewers bring their own rich imaginations to interact with the work. Hesitant to elaborate on his original intentions, Segal stated:

> I've been limiting my own conversations. I've dropped those references. What's more important for me is exactly what you've been encouraging your students to do to have their own responses. I don't want to dictate.[20]

Nevertheless, Segal would be disappointed if the viewer missed the connections of his work to biblical traditions. Dimensions of transcendence derive from sensing the connections that Holocaust victims and contemporary viewers, as well as models for the sculpture, have to biblical and historical religious thoughts. Segal stressed that the references to biblical figures were ways for him to honor the rich spiritual life of the Holocaust victims who themselves are to be seen as more than merely dead forms. It was important, he said,

> To make some kind of reference to the mental life of these people . . . who had been strongly connected with a complicated history—a history of spiritual invention—transcendent thought. This poverty stricken mass of dirt that was dead had this connection with an incredible amount of spiritual energy. This connection is what I was after. How you do it we've been talking about that. It was quite important that this whole other aura take place . . . an intensely felt spiritual life.[21]

Segal's attempt to do justice to the rich mental life not only of the victims and the viewers but also of his models results in the multiplicity of interpretations. His description of his creative process reveals how he honors and incorporates the bodies and minds of his models:

> What I was doing was number one carefully choosing my models. They had to have the physical appearance I was interested in; but they also had to have a mental set. They had to have a very lively internal life of their own: loved art, loved reading, and loved ideas. And then we talked about what they were doing. Then they were telling me their ideas of death. They were telling me all these things that occurred to them and then finally it became very simple. We got into

the pose. I couldn't violate their ideas because here are sensitive people, very bright with their own memories, very strong convictions, and their own ideas about what had happened. Some people had never seen death, some had. We were talking about the Bible, all the relevant things.[22]

This process was informed by Segal's original intentions: "I told them what I was thinking of; and they would think about it."[23] It was their thinking, however, which enlarged the associations.

Reflecting on how his postmodern art differs from premodern art with respect to the use of biblical subject, Segal agreed that the postmodern expressions are less explicit, less clear, more ambiguous, more tacit in some ways:

Yes. Yes. I think that what happens is the ambiguity is cultivated because we have now a strong rejection of deliberate dogma. At least for me that's true. . . . If there is nobody up there on some pedestal or altar place telling us what's right and wrong, what's good and bad, what we should be doing in our time, we are forced to figure it out for ourselves. And not only that but because of the twentieth century, machinery, television, satellites, etc., we talk to a lot of different kinds of people; we're not as narrow or parochial. I think that intelligent people from everywhere want to find or are fumbling for some universal ground, which is why I cheerfully put the cruciform into this awful terrible Jewish experience.[24]

He also sees the rich background upon which artists now draw as contributing to the differences between premodern and postmodern art. His own knowledge of so much art history makes it difficult to trace both his tacit and explicit intentions. Segal stated,

> It's because of this very fact that we have this tumble of thoughts (these up and down feelings). The realism of the twentieth century has to do with the freedom to explore all these areas. That's why twentieth century religious art is different.[25]

On the differences between postmodern and premodern use of the human figure in art, Segal stressed how the postmodern use engages the viewer in a range of different responses.

> Quite simply, all right, let's use *The Holocaust* as an example. It's at a physical space. When you first come to it, you look down. You see it from the top; you walk down a ramp or steps. You can walk into the spaces. At one point, you are behind the fence; and psychologically you are either a prisoner or a guard. You are within the camp. But on the outside, you are either a visitor or allied soldier. . . . As you walk around the piece, you are in a different psychological place; so that's not common. That's twentieth century. In the past, let's say you take a medieval church, there was either a stained glass window all the way up there with an enormous amount of empty space in the nave or there were paintings on the side. The

paintings were flat; the sculptures were in niches.
They are part of the architectural scheme. Paintings or sculpture had their proper places in architecture. Sculpture used to be placed on a pedestal
to make it different from daily space. In my own
work, I embrace daily space; and I try to set up
something that is quite intense but in daily space
that I can walk into and walk around and have all
these whole range of responses. When you actually physically walk around to different parts of
the sculpture, there are different experiences.[26]

In a letter to George Segal, French art critic and editor of
DOMUS Pierre Restany expressed how seeing Segal's *The
Holocaust* affects one who takes the time to look carefully.

Your Holocaust piece gave me one of the deepest
emotions of my life. It is not only a beautiful piece
of narrative sculpture, it is above all a great contri-
bution to the history of mankind, the most powerful catalyst for our memories. I will never forget
the impression which caught me in the beautiful
site of the Legion of Honour's Palace in San Francisco. Very few sculptors can give us such a feeling
of noble humanity and celebration of life beyond
the death, the injustice, the genocide. You are
one of those rare artists, George, and among the
greatest, because you are fundamentally
human.[27]

In reflecting on that letter and particularly the phrase
"celebration of life," Segal confirmed the celebration element that Restany sees in *The Holocaust.*

I thought very hard about that. I wanted that in.
It is a necessary element. I hate being a mourner.
It's almost incredibly difficult to begin to deal
with the fact of the holocaust unless there is some
celebration of life or some strong statement of the
value of continuing life. There has to be some
inhibition to taking life cheaply.[28]

Segal acknowledges that in *The Holocaust*, "I do intend a
certain kind of gentleness and love."[29] Many viewers speak
about the deep healing that Segal's *The Holocaust* communicates. When first seeing the plaster model of the work in
Segal's New Jersey studio, Jane Dillenberger noted, "Why
George, it is about love." The interrelating among figures
in the sculpture also invites an interrelating with the
viewer. John Dillenberger said to Segal, "They are so
peaceful." Segal responded, "They ought to be peaceful,
they have been dead for over forty years." Then Segal
added, "They forgave us a long time ago; but we have not
yet forgiven them."[30] In Segal's work we have forgiving
without forgetting.

Pondering Segal's words, I remembered a woman whose
husband died. She responded, "I will never forgive him for
dying and leaving me alone." For Segal to say of Holocaust
victims, "We have not yet forgiven them" is analogous to
the woman saying she had not forgiven her husband for
dying. Survivors are left without the company of those who
died. With the Holocaust, there is the added dimension of
guilt felt by the living who could have done more to save
the victims but instead must live with a memory of their
own limitations. Jews could understandably continue to
blame Christians who were in positions to do more to help

Jews escape. Segal's inclusion of a Christ figure in his work may be read as a gesture of forgiveness toward Christians and in itself an act transcending the boundaries of faith traditions.

Positive and negative criticisms of Segal's *The Holocaust* reveal other dimensions of transcendence in art. In *J.A.C.O.B.S. Letter,* Andrea Liss argued, "Silence has been considered the most appropriate and respectful response to the unfathomable horror of the Holocaust."[31] Her position is not to be confused with the argument that the Holocaust reveals the death of God, that art is no longer possible, and that silence is the response to despair. For her and for others, the concern is that embodiments of the Holocaust in art domesticate or reduce its impact. There is such liveliness in the very materials an artist shapes (whether those materials be words or paint or metal) that they produce a positive quality even when portraying the most horrorifying subject matter. Elie Wiesel's response to Samuel Beckett may be remembered: "Even to write about despair is a step beyond despair."[32]

If such an event is to be portrayed, others argue that only abstraction avoids such domestication. In *J.A.C.O.B.S. Letter,* John Felstiner ascribes such a view to art historian Peter Selz.

> Professor Selz holds, convincingly, that only an abstract approach, not a representational one, can work in our time. The average visitor to a realistically styled Holocaust sculpture—however horrifying the image—might too readily assimilate an event that in scale and detail ruptured all similarity to human experience. And yet what sort

of abstract form, facing what sort of viewer, could convey this unimaginable event? Maybe a single small bar of granite into which every single name of all the millions murdered has been engraved, one on top of the next—in effect, then, a blank stone or no stone left at all.[33]

Others argued that monumental art must be larger-than-life.[34] Others reported views that the suffering is not graphic enough.[35] Edward Rodati objected to so many healthy bodies in the work:

a group of relatively healthy-looking human bodies which appear to be sunbathing on a nude beach. They have none of the physical appearance of the hideously emaciated corpses and of the survivors discovered in Buchenwald, Dachau or Bergen-Belsen by the liberating Allied armies.[36]

Only the heap of four bodies in the sculpture comes close to the concentration camp photographs that Segal studied. He explains why his work did not mirror more of such photos:

I must have looked at a thousand photographs . . . and I was struck by the obscenity of the disorder, the heaping of the bodies. In most countries, there is a ritual order at funerals. The corpses are carefully composed, and there is a ritual of grieving. Here was a decision by a modern state to perform official murder of an entire race. The indignity of the heaping, the total disregard for

death, spoke of insanity. . . . If I were to recreate
the chaos . . . I'd have to use the Nazi brutality
and contempt to arrive at a solution. I don't think
it is the function of the artist to repeat that kind of
bankrupt frame of mind. It is much more important to make room for the private tendrils of response everywhere.[37]

Art historian David Wright complained that the figures
were unacceptable because Segal's models were not in an
advanced state of anorexia nervosa to approximate the emaciated concentration camp victims.[38] Segal has noted "that
the trains delivered enormous crowds of Jews who were
tricked into the disinfecting showers and were gassed.
There could be bodies, I reasoned, that were of normal size
as well as thin."[39] While the Yad Vatshem Holocaust memorial in Jerusalem is filled with photographs of hopeless,
isolated, and emaciated persons reflecting the state of many
in the concentration camps, Segal goes beyond mirroring
the photographs and reveals hope through relationships.
Such interrelationships were possible in the camps as Victor Frankl witnessed.[40]

Hopeful human figures and references to Jewish and
Christian literature appear frequently in the works of another contemporary Jewish artist, Alice Lok Cahana. A
survivor of Auschwitz, she creates paintings incorporating
the poetry and rituals which witnessed to faith in the
camps. She associates the rectangular shape of a large
painting with the top of a dining table and titles it *Sabbath
In Auschwitz (Homage to Edith)* (1985: Private Collection).
In that work, she includes Hebrew excerpts from the *Hag-
gadah* (the Passover prayerbook), abstract candles, and faint

outlines of human figures. The Hebrew passages speak of God's strong arm that brings the people out from Egypt: a theme that gave hope to Alice Lok Cahana in the camp.[41]

Barbara Rose notes a connection of Cahana's work to Robert Rauschenberg's collaged "combine" paintings.[42] In *Homage To Raoul Wallenberg* (1984–85: Private Collection), many narrative qualities are present: a photograph of Wallenberg, some of the papers that the Swedish diplomat issued to save a hundred thousand Jews in Budapest, photographs of persons in the camps, and an excerpt from the Dead Sea scrolls. Through her inclusion of fragments from ancient Hebrew writings, Cahana intends to remind us of our connections to historic Jewish culture, which survives much as Segal's inclusion of biblical figures in *The Holocaust* has to do with survival; and her inclusion of crosses in some of her paintings is a gesture of forgiveness to Christians as is Segal's inclusion of the cruciform in *The Holocaust*.[43] The photographs and shapes of persons witness to her view that "one man can make a difference, that the individual can and must act."[44]

There has been positive response to a dimension that could have evoked criticism of Segal from Jewish communities: the inclusion of cruciform shapes as well as other overt references to Christ such as the figures reminiscent of crucifixion and deposition scenes. One reviewer noted "the marks on the body of one man bring to mind the sores on the Christ in Grünewald's *Isenheim Altarpiece*—the most powerful of all representations of Christ as Man of Sorrows and certainly the most appropriate image of Christ for this subject and perhaps for the modern age."[45] A generation ago, proposing the inclusion of a cross in a memorial to the Holocaust was considered offensive to Jewish sensibilities.

Today Segal's *The Holocaust* can be praised in Jewish publications because it transcends any one tradition:

> it is beyond control and beyond anticipation. Like all great and surprising art (simplistic in conception, stunning in actuality), it is beyond the pale of ownership. It transcends the particularity of the Jewish holocaust, even as it ennobles it.[46]

In affirming transcendence where the individual connects with others and to a center beyond himself or herself, Segal's postmodern construction differs sharply from Mark Taylor's postmodern a/theology. Based on the method of deconstruction, Taylor's work begins with the modernist elimination of any meaningful sense of place or time or transcendence; and so, history becomes a/history and theology becomes a/theology. In his *Erring: A Postmodern A/Theology*, Taylor writes:

> Postmodernism opens with the sense of *irrevocable* loss and *incurable* fault. This wound is inflicted by the overwhelming awareness of death— a death that "begins" with the death of God and "ends" with the death of ourselves. We are in a time between times and a "place which is no place."[47]

Massive death in the twentieth-century Holocaust gave impetus to the death of God a/theology. Taylor's postmodern a/theology begins with the modern sense of "loss" and takes its cue from that which has been lost. For a/theology, lost is the possibility of relating to anything beyond self; and even the self is deconstructed. In contrast, postmodern art does not take its cue from what has been lost, but from what has been gained by de-absolutizing the Cartesian self and the dichotomous categories of modernism.

Postmodern art moves beyond mind/body and subject/ object dichotomies which were a part of René Descartes's seventeenth-century thinking and reconnects us to wider worlds and histories as in George Segal's art. Charles Jencks calls such connections a chief characteristic of postmodern art:

> For the Modernist predicament, often epitomized in Yeat's words "Things fall apart; the center cannot hold" we have the dialectical answer "Things fall together, and there is no center, but connections." Or in E. M. Forster's words "connect, only connect."[48]

Jencks asserts, "Contrary to common belief . . . postmodernism is neither anti-Modern nor reactionary," but it "puts Positivism in its place" and begins a revolution "without breaking anything more than a few eggheads."[49]

Segal's work goes further than Jencks's characterization of postmodern art; for *The Holocaust* constructively moves beyond deconstruction and toward an awareness of transcendence in which there are not only connections but suggestions of a center beyond the individual. The perceptions of transcendence come through human bodies expressing biblical subject matter and allowing multiple interpretations and interfaith appreciation.

Stephen De Staebler's Sculptures: Religious Forms of Graceful Aging, Dying, and Rising

*W*hile sculptor Stephen De Staebler (b. 1933) creates some works with overt religious subject matter, he offers a much larger body of work that is concerned with transcendence by virtue of form rather than subject matter. His sculptures express and help one experience transcendence, a sense of the other beyond oneself. Sensing transcendence through the form of art increases the range of visual art explored in theology.

De Staebler's works are often religious in form without being religious in subject matter. Forms bore theological meaning in earlier periods' art which contained religious subject matter. Such works may usually be considered religious by virtue of their subject matter; nevertheless, profound theological significance in visual art may be borne directly by their forms. In the Renaissance perspective, the viewers of art stand supreme at the center of a universe. Other objects and persons appear smaller in a painting's background and larger in the foreground. Through reverse and multiple perspectives of Greek and Russian icons, viewers are in a modest place. Persons and objects are smaller in the foreground and larger in the middle ground or background. Viewers reshape their thinking to relate meaningfully to a center beyond themselves.

The shift from a Renaissance perspective to the icons's reverse perspective is like the shift in thinking invited by Jesus's parables.[1] Before hearing the parable of the Good Samaritan, a man self-centeredly asks, "What shall I do to inherit eternal life?" In conversation with Jesus, the man begins to shift his focus away from himself by asking, "Who is my neighbor?" By the end of the parable, the man does not speak of himself but speaks only of "the one who showed mercy" on another person (Luke 10:25–37).

Reverse and multiple perspectives reveal the theologies of Eastern Orthodox Christian icons and El Greco's art. Some scholars have described how such perspectives inform the development of cubism and other techniques in modern art; and so, attention to these forms develops an appreciation for modern art as theological.[2] Considering visual art works as theological expressions is normative in Eastern Orthodox Christian churches where paintings and words are both affirmed as equally needed ways of communicating the Word.

Andrei Rublev's *The Holy Trinity* (1411: Tretyekov Gallery, Moscow) (fig. 10) is called the icon of icons and the highest statement of theology in the Russian Orthodox Church.[3] Created around 1411, this icon depicts the three angels of Genesis 18:1-8. While that story speaks of Abraham's hospitality to strangers, the Eastern Orthodox Christian tradition treated the three angels as prefigurations of

10. Andrei Rublev, *The Holy Trinity*, 1411. Tetreyekov Gallery, Moscow.

11. El Greco, *Saint Francis*, c. 1590–1604. Oil on canvas. 92.6 × 74.6 cm. Robert A. Waller Memorial Fund, 1935.372. Photograph © 1991, The Art Institute of Chicago. All Rights Reserved.

the Trinity and the meal as Communion. Icons based on that biblical text explored the theological dynamics of the Trinity and Communion that model how the believer is to live in community with God and others.

In an unknown artist's slightly earlier version of this theme titled *Old Testament Trinity* (1410: Russian Museum, Leningrad), reverse perspective is evident as the central angel behind the table and in the background is obviously larger than the two foreground angels seated at the sides of the table. In the foreground are the smaller figures of Abraham and Sarah serving the meal. In Rublev's version, the central background figure is subtly larger than the two angels in the foreground while Abraham and Sarah have been eliminated.

Like the subtle cubism of many of Paul Cézanne's paintings of fruit on a table such as *Still Life With Fruit Basket* (1888–90: Louvre, Paris), Rublev's work allows for multiple perspectives that further undermine a viewer's sense of standing at one central fixed point. One sees the table top (as if one were looking down on it) at the same time that one sees its front and underneath it (as if one were standing in front of it or below it). Similarly, one sees the cup from the top and from the front.

The combination of reverse and multiple perspectives disorients the viewer and causes a slight dizziness. As historical theologian Margaret R. Miles notes, "a person grasps God's transcendence by the perception of an image that dizzies and before which her or his breath is taken away."[4] Such an experience unsettles one and shows one that he or she is not the center of the world. For Christians, transcendence begins when one senses the other who is beyond oneself and makes one aware of one's finitude.

Having made one aware of the limitations in any one fixed viewpoint, Rublev's icon then invites movement into more dynamic relationships within a community. These dynamics become evident when trying to fix attention on just one of the three figures portrayed. Such a fixation is impossible to maintain for all of the figures are looking away from themselves and calling attention to the others as their eyes, heads, and bodies incline toward others. If one focuses on the figure to one's left, he is looking toward the figure to one's right. That figure to one's right is looking back toward the figure on one's left. Similarly the coloration of the garments results in attention being drawn from one figure to another. The blue of the tunic on the figure to one's left is relatively faint while the blue is more intense in the figure's tunic on one's right and is most intense in the central figure's outer garment. That central figure looks to one's left and keeps one's attention moving.

Healthy relationships in community are modeled by such avoidance of fixation on any one other person. Those dynamics are also designed to avoid theological heresy; for "heresy is a kind of picking and choosing, a denial of the wholeness and fullness of the faith."[5] Most heresies result when people pick one valid doctrine but stress it to the exclusion of other valid doctrines. Heresy, like idolatry, is mistaking the part for the whole. Such preoccupation with any one figure in the Trinity is prevented by the dynamics in Rublev's icon.

Interpreters argue as to whether the central figure is God or Christ; but they agree the figure to the viewer's right is the Holy Spirit. All three figures appear taller than the average person. They would evidently be nine or ten heads high if they were standing, whereas the average person is six or seven heads high. That seeming "distortion" is how persons appear when they are far above us. This elongation of the figures is another aspect of multiple perspectives in icons, also evident in El Greco's paintings. For example, in *St. Francis* (c. 1590–1604: The Art Institute of Chicago) (fig. 11), the kneeling Francis would be more than ten heads high if he stood up. In his native Crete, El Greco learned the dynamics of icon painting such as reverse perspective, which is evident in the book whose far edge is longer than its near edge. In fact, the far leg of the crucifix is longer than the near leg in *St. Francis*. From El Greco, some modern artists have learned reverse and multiple perspectives that present theological dimensions in modern art.[6] So we may discover theological significance in visual art forms, although different forms may bear different theological perceptions as indicated by art historian Joshua Taylor's method detailed in chapter 4.

In Stephen De Staebler's sculptures, the forms which embody incompletion and suffering also express the individual's capacities to relate to others beyond himself or herself. Such incompletion and suffering evoke the viewer's empathy and self-transcendence. Drawing on De Staebler's own words in an earlier published conversation with Diane Apostolos-Cappadona,[7] Donald Kuspit affirms that the sculptor's concern with suffering identifies his art as religious.

> It is a religious art form. De Staebler has said that "religion addresses suffering," and that art tries "to restructure reality so that we can live with the suffering." He wants to create a modern religious art, utilizing archaic forms for an "archaic" pur-

pose: the articulation and remediation of suffering.[8]

With De Staebler works, transcendence does not eliminate the body's suffering but presents it as the condition for transcendence. In his early *Crucifix* (1968: Holy Spirit Chapel, Newman Hall, Berkeley) (fig. 12), Christ is suffering and being born at the same time. The largely undefined figure looks as if it is thrusting forward from the wall. The artist confirmed the simultaneity of suffering and transcendence.

> That would really be what was hoped for. The priest . . . and I talked about this, how to establish some impending sense of transcendence and resurrection without sacrificing the suffering.[9]

De Staebler talks about "separateness and fusion working simultaneously" in his art.[10]

His works avoid an idealization of the whole human form and instead affirm transcendence through fragmented bodies such as *Seated Woman With Oval Head* (1981: Private Collection) (fig. 14). Such arrangement of fragments asserts that the human being "is not a whole or a unity but an idiosyncratic bundle of contradictions."[11]

When students sit in the stoneware clay chairs of *Seating Environment* (1970: University Art Museum, Berkeley), each finds the chair which best fits his or her own body. These seats are highly individuated places and not as similar as they first appear. The students report that their own different body shapes feel affirmed by the experience of finding a fitting chair. That affirmation is especially appreci-

12. Stephen De Staebler, *Crucifix*, 1968. Stoneware clay. 8×7 feet. Holy Spirit Parish, Newman Hall, Berkeley, California. Courtesy Stephen De Staebler.

ated by those students whose bodies would not win them awards in our "body conscious" culture.

De Staebler's sculptures of the human body have similar effects. Replicating *Seated Woman With Oval Head* with their own bodies, students sit on the edge of desk tops or counters so that the lower legs hang straight down from the upper legs which are slanted down at a forty-five degree angle. Their feet are flexed with toes pointing toward the ground; and the left foot appears in front. They hold their torsos and heads erect, facing straight forward. This is not an easy position to maintain as students become aware of a precarious balance. One ballet dancer reported that her upper torso, head, and feet felt like she was on pointe, although her legs defied that feeling. Should they lean forward, they feel as if they will fall. The figure is as far forward as is possible without falling. In that position, students feel a dignity that comes from several factors: the erect upper body and head, the balance of the body, and the sensation of being on pointe or at least being as far forward as possible. This kinesthetic knowledge was in contrast to what students initially thought about the sculpted figure which had appeared relaxed or hopelessly shattered on first viewing. The lack of arms added to the sense of dignity and historic worth as the work resonated with their memory of much surviving classical art.

Nevertheless, De Staebler's work differs from such classical sculpture as two students observed. These two permanently disabled students reported that they felt affirmed by De Staebler's sculpture with its fragmented legs, no arms, and fragile balance. For them, this work of art expresses the condition of bodily brokenness, yet it does not decry this human condition but deeply affirms it. In contrast, their

14. Stephen De Staebler, *Seated Woman with Oval Head*, 1981. Cast
bronze A.P. 68 × 23 × 25½ inches. Private Collection. Photograph by
Scott McCue. Courtesy Stephen De Staebler.

experience of classical sculpture had made them feel hopelessly inadequate. They said their bodies could never measure up to the beauty and balance of those classical nudes.
Their previous experience of broken bodies in sculpture
was in art of the 1950s and 1960s protesting some larger
social problems rather than appreciating disabled bodies.

To allow for graceful aging and deeper empathizing with
others, De Staebler rejects the idealization of the body.

> I think that idealization of the body has been a
> very questionable enterprise at best because at its
> extreme what it leads to is a kind of glorification of
> youth which just doesn't allow for graceful
> aging. [12]

He continued, "the only thing that keeps us from being
monsters as a species is acknowledgement of our own
finitude."[13] He spoke of incomplete bodies and not broken
bodies. The incomplete forms allow a deeper conversation
between the viewer and the art work.

> It helps bridge the gulf when the other person or
> the image in the art is less complete. I think
> everyone feels inadequacies, incompleteness; and
> of course the worst of society is trying to pretend
> you do not have these limitations, violating, possi-
> bly irreparably, your own uniqueness, which is
> largely a factor of incompleteness. We are who we
> are not so much because of what we have or are
> endowed with but because of what we are not
> endowed with. To have an image which is less
> than fully endowed is a basis for empathy, but not

easy to accept if the person who is the viewer wants to deny that he has any limitations. It's like saying, O.K., we can have a dialogue if we agree we both have limitations. Then we can go from there. And that is really the basis of mature interpersonal relationships, isn't it, when you think about it?[14]

His sculptures are frontal even if they are only part of the body: *Standing Man with Outstretched Arm II* (1989: Private Collection) (fig. 16). The frontal presentation of the sculptures' bodies reminds the viewer of his or her limitations, and the mystery of the other and the unknown. Speaking of the frontality of his sculpture, De Staebler continued.

I'm really taken by frontal imagery, I think, because I identify so much with my own body. The human body has a frontal orientation for life: our eyes are on one side; all our senses are oriented toward the front. And we know life through this frontality. One of the things that no one really wants to talk that much about is this horrible blind spot that we've got behind us. We have to go through all waking life with the unknown behind us. It's part of the anxiety of being a creature, I suppose, because you don't know what threat may be from behind. Certain animals, you know, have their eyes to the sides to overcome the problem of frontality. The obverse of frontality is the unknown. You have a mystery always implicit in any fixed point of view. If you're gazing this way, the other way is the dark.[15]

16. Stephen De Staebler, *Standing Man with Outstretched Arm II*, 1989. Bronze AP/UC. 95¼ × 49 × 26⅜ inches. Private Collection. Photograph by Scott McCue. Courtesy Stephen De Staebler.

The frontal form suggests also an engagement or commitment with another person such as occurs at a dinner party through face-to-face conversation. De Staebler contrasts such a dinner tête-à-tête with the uncommitted talk at a cocktail party where a face-to-face stance is often avoided in favor of standing at oblique angles to be able to look beyond the person to see if someone more interesting is coming. De Staebler expands on this imagery.

> The ground rule of a cocktail party is never to become engaged or never to be cornered so that you can't slip away before a situation becomes less than enjoyable or threatening; whereas at a dinner party, you can't very well edge your chair over and sit next to the other guy.[16]

There are varieties of the frontal presentation. As in *Bisected Woman Standing* (1982: Private Collection), De Staebler's sculptured figures avoid articulation of eyes and faces or have no heads; and his masks similarly avoid articulation of the eyes as, for example, in *Pink-Striped Face* (1975: Private Collection) (fig. 17). This frontal presentation evokes a sense of transcendence and may remind the viewer of the frontality of the Christ Pantocrator found in Eastern Orthodox churches. However, De Staebler's use of frontality differs in significant ways, including the fundamental accessibility of his sculptures. He works to avoid the dominance exemplified by the *Christ Pantocrator* (11th century; Monastery at Daphne, Greece) (fig. 18), which he sees as too confrontational. His aim is rather to invite the viewer into a conversation between equals that could easily become a monologue dominated by the sculpture if the

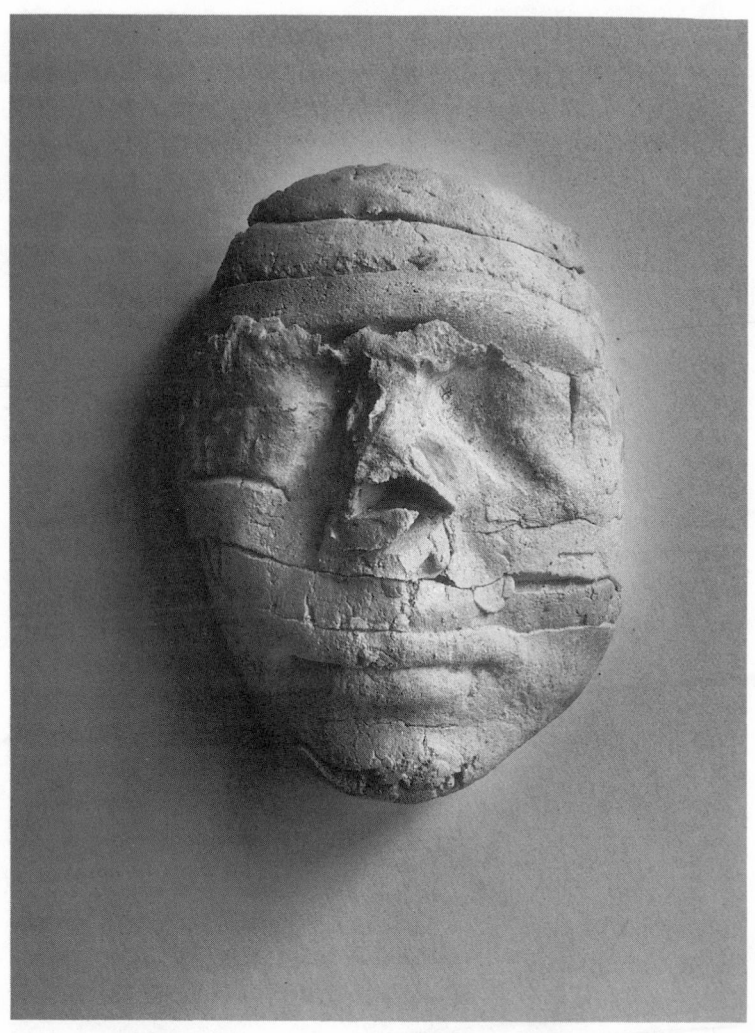

17. Stephen De Staebler, *Pink-striped Face*, 1975. Fired clay. 6½ × 5 × 3 inches. Private Collection. Photograph by Susan Felter. Courtesy Stephen De Staebler.

18. *Pantocrator*, 11th century. Monastery at Daphni, Greece. Courtesy of the Byzantine Photograph Collection, © 1991, Dumbarton Oaks, Washington, D.C. (A.76.44 (R)).

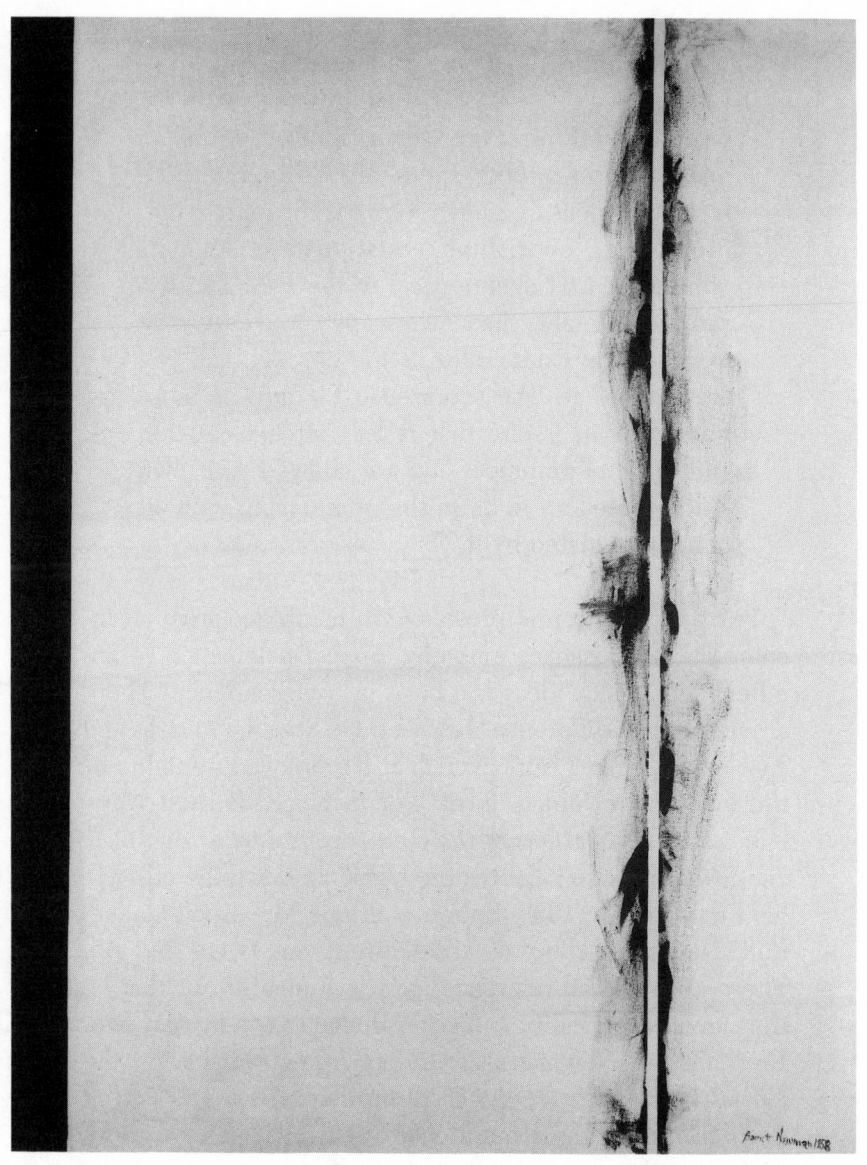

19. Barnett Newman, *First Station*, 1958. Magna on canvas. 77⅞ × 60½ inches. Robert and Jane Meyerhoff Collection, National Gallery of Art, Washington, D.C. (1986.65.1 (PA)).

eyes were detailed. De Staebler likens the frontal presentation of his sculptures to a nurturing relationship.

> Even if you think of the nurturing relationship, an infant with its mother, there's frontality; but there is not eye-focus frontality. There is the embracing, protecting, nourishing, relationship. And its oblique: it isn't symmetrical to the eye. The Byzantine frontality had no escape. You enter the world of the Pantocrator or the crucifix; and you are held by it. The experience I would be more interested in is one that is less of confrontation and more of embrace. You are allowed your own kind of freedom to be in the relationship without being dominated by it.[17]

Further, this frontal presentation combined with an incomplete body evokes empathy. Such participation in another's feelings or ideas is a basis of transcendence. There are instructive differences between De Staebler's works and earlier modern art works which also employed frontality or the incomplete human form. For instance, Barnett Newman's abstract *Stations of the Cross* are frontal as the black zip down one side balances the black zip down the other in his *First Station* (1958: Robert and Jane Meyerhoff Collection, National Gallery of Art, Washington, D.C.) (fig. 19). There are residual references to the human form, that is, the canvas's verticality and equivalence to the human size. Frontality in Newman's art differs from frontality in the *Christ Pantocrator* at the Daphne monastery. The *Christ Pantocrator* evokes a hierarchal world in which the work dictates to the viewer, while Newman's painting when hung at the proper height from the floor engages the viewer "in a conversation as if with another human being. The work of art and the viewer are transformed into conversation partners."[18] The black zips suggest a suffering that may engage the viewer's empathy. De Staebler acknowledged some similarities, but then noted, "You aren't required to empathize with Newman's image; but it doesn't prevent it."[19]

De Staebler's sculptures also differ from earlier frontal works featuring the overt human body. If one compares De Staebler's *Seated Man with Winged Head* (1981: Private Collection) (fig. 15) with Leonard Baskin's *Hydrogen Man* (1954; Private Collection), the incompleteness or finitiude found in De Staebler's work is an affirmation; but the incompletion in Baskin's work reveals flaws to be decried in the world.[20]

As the differently abled students noted, De Staebler's works were the first seen that had raised the issues of finitude or bodily incompleteness in an affirmative manner. They felt a dignity not experienced in others's works. De Staebler responded.

> That is really gratifying to hear, Doug. I know now consciously that that is what I am trying to come to terms with. I know that what we've been talking around is an extremely personal issue with me; and I suppose it is for anyone who is not rejecting or denying the ultimate end of us all.[21]

Like De Staebler, all human beings have close relatives or friends who are physically deteriorating or dying as all will. De Staebler's works witness to an integrity and persistence of individual personality even in the face of such bodily deterioration or death.

The sense of a persisting personality is evident in his

15. Stephen De Staebler, *Seated Man with Winged Head*, 1981. Cast bronze AP. 67½ × 23 × 26 inches. Private Collection. Photograph by Scott McCue. Courtesy Stephen De Staebler.

angel works, such as *Left Sided Angel* (1986: Iowa State University, Ames) or *Right Sided Angel* (1986: Private Collection) or *Archangel* (1987: Private Collection) (fig. 20) where the lower part of the body, so detailed in many of his earlier works, is less articulated. There is far less of a sense of gravity than in his previous works as these angels no longer seem bound down to the earth. In *Archangel*, the foot is detached; like an empty tomb, the base shows the impressions of what was once present but is now gone. The right leg is gone; but a mold for it remains. The torso remains prominent; above the left shoulder looms a large extension which could be a wing or some other formation or transformation of the person into an as yet unknown shape.

A further transformation is evident in De Staebler's 1986–87 light sculpture and water sculpture for the New Harmony Inn and Conference Center, New Harmony, Indiana.[22] In De Staebler's *The Vision of St. Benedict* (1986–87: New Harmony Inn Conference Center, New Harmony) (fig. 21), negative space is created through a vertical groove in the wall. In a number of ways, a persistence of the individual human is suggested. De Staebler related that the width and depth of his own body fits into the groove, although the groove is many times taller than a human form. He agreed that the verticality of the work suggests the human form. As the torso continued to be a very prominent section throughout his works, so the upper central section of the groove was the deepest and therefore most prominent when lights illumined the wall from either side above the work and created shadows in the groove. At the bottom or top where the groove tapers to become flush with the wall, there are no shadows; but in the upper central section (where the groove is deepest), the shadows are prominent and give the impression of a transforming presence. De Staebler said, "where the individuation comes in is in the changing light and shadow patterns that are generated by its shape."[23]

His art, then, has moved beyond the corporeal existence of an individual to a later shape of a person's soul. De Staebler discussed the difference.

> First of all, we're talking about a negative, a void, which is only brought to life by the shadows that it generates; so it's a kind of negation of mass. And this of course is quite different from seeing a corporeal effigy which is in space and you identify with it.[24]

The De Staebler works in New Harmony are technologically anticipated in part by his *Water Sculpture* (1972: Concord Station of Bay Area Rapid Transit District, Concord) and his *Wall Canyon* (1976–77: Embarcadero Station of Bay Area Rapid Transit District, San Francisco). In his New Harmony light sculpture, the sense of individual soul is suggested by the description of St. Benedict's vision that inspired Jane Blaffer Owen both to conceive of the wall in a conference center dedicated to St. Benedict and to ask De Staebler to do the sculptural treatment of the wall. She supplied De Staebler with this description of the saint's vision.

> The brethren were already asleep but Benedict was still awake. Suddenly, in the depth of the night, he beheld a light pouring forth from the sky, dispelling the darkness and shining with such

20. Stephen De Staebler, *Archangel*, 1987. Bronze AP. 119 × 26½ × 34½ inches. Private Collection. Photograph by Scott McCue. Courtesy Stephen De Staebler.

brightness that it would have outshone the light of
day. Before his very eyes, the whole world
seemed to be gathered into a single sunbeam.
Benedict then beheld, in a ball of fire, the soul of
Germanus, Bishop of Capua, borne to Heaven by
angels. . . . This vision gives Gregory the oppor-
tunity to insert a homily on contemplation, which
in the light of God opens wide the soul, transports
it above itself and reveals to it in miniature the
whole of creation.[25]

On a smaller scale, the outdoor *Water Sculpture* (1986–
87: New Harmony Inn Cloister, New Harmony) resonates
with the indoor light sculpture. The groove in the vertical
fountain deepens as one moves up the work toward the
center so that shadows created by the sun are most prominent in the upper middle. Water as well as light makes the
viewer aware of a changing presence during the day; and
the abundant waters of the fountain provide a billowing
cloud like column. At night, the lighting transforms the
work into a pillar of fire. One may remember passages from
Exodus and Deuteronomy about the divine presence in the
pillar of cloud by day and pillar of fire by night.

Through the incompleteness and frontality of his human
figures, and through the transformations of his angel, light,
and water sculptures, De Staebler maintains a tension between "separateness" and "fusion." He sees those terms as
paralleling Joshua Taylor's distinctions between "communitive" and "unitive" art forms which are discussed in chapter 4.[26] De Staebler read Taylor's views and found them
helpful in seeing religious dimensions in works without
overt religious subject matter.

21. Stephen De Stabler, *The Model for The Vision of St. Benedict*, 1988.
For the New Harmony Inn Conference Center, New Harmony, Indiana.
Collection of the Artist. Courtesy Stephen De Staebler.

Much of Stephen De Staebler's art expresses what he calls separateness and what Taylor called communitive will to fellowship; but there is as well what De Staebler calls fusion and what Taylor called a unitive will to form. As a Princeton University religion major who wrote his undergraduate thesis on St. Francis, De Staebler recalls associating these different forms with Western and Eastern religions.

> I had a teacher who referred to the quest of seeing the face of God as positive mysticism, and the quest of being absorbed in God as negative mysticism. The Eastern orientation is essentially female: Hinduism and Buddhism as involved with the nothingness of absorption, the drop of water into the ocean. In Christianity, with both Hebraic and Greek thought behind it, individuality is not obliterated but is consciously in relationship with God. That kind of relationship with ultimate reality leads to a different understanding of life and requires a different type of personality from the one that is seeking absorption.[27]

In his sculptures, De Staebler is concerned to maintain an equilibrium between separateness and fusion.[28] While the separateness may be more evident, he notes his concern for fusion: "it's that quality of having an order which is very unapparent—which is submerged in the form—that really satisfied me. And that's what the experience of nature is."[29] The strong communitive character of most of his works suggests his grounding in Judeo-Christian traditions.

Stephen De Staebler's artistic vision is most powerfully

rendered in his *Pietà* (1989: The Roofless Church, New Harmony) (fig. 22) commissioned by Jane Blaffer Owen. This life-sized bronze sculpture resonates with but differs from Michelangelo's *Rondanini Pietà* (1564: Castello Sforesca, Milan) (fig. 23). For example, De Staebler's two standing figures merge by overlapping at the sides; but the back of Michelangelo's Christ merges with the front of Mary. Only two legs are visible in De Staebler's work where the left leg recedes and appears to have suffered as the right leg moves forward in robust life. While we may intially think of the left leg as Christ's and the right leg as Mary's, the figures are more merged than that; and one may note a hole in each foot and a wound in the right side of the body. The head of Christ emerges at the level of his mother's left breast. That head is bowed and bald. Above the mother's head emerges an ambiguous shape which could be a nimbus, a flame, or an as yet unrealized form into which the bodies are being transformed. The green tones in the lower parts of the sculpture give way to increasingly gold tones in the upper parts.

Interpretations surfaced as Stephen De Staebler reflected in the presence of his *Pietà* at the Artworks Foundry in Berkeley, California, where it was cast. He stressed his concern for recognition of the earth as one's connection to the sacred.

> It is using earth forms like fractured stone . . . making it the connection with the divine, which I think really is the secret anyway. The earth is sacred. We have lost sight of it. Now we really know because we are so close to extinction; and the ecological disasters are multiplying. But sym-

22. Stephen De Staebler, *Pieta*, 1988. Bronze AP. 92 × 17¼ × 27 inches. The Roofless Church, New Harmony, Indiana. Photograph by Scott McCue. Courtesy Stephen De Staebler.

23. Michelangelo, *Rondanini Pieta*, 1564. Marble. 63⅜ inches high.
Castello Sforesca, Milan. Courtesy Alinari/Art Resource, New York.

bolically, winged flame lifting the figure of mother and child upward speaks to what the earth is made of.[30]

Human connection to the earth is emphasized by De Staebler in the absence of arms and in the erosion of the left leg.

> I want to express the quality of erosion in the loss of limbs over time and the rooting of the figure to the earth in time, so that it becomes in its way an extension of earth, which we are. We only exist by the grace of the earth's nature. So what you see here is this feeling of an eroded separation from something larger in time. . . . I hope that for the person who isn't too literal this will also have that connotation of being connected in time to creation.[31]

He observed that missing limbs are easily accepted when viewers see classical sculpture or Renaissance works inspired by classical sculptures. Anticipating some people's criticisms for the lack of arms in his work, he advised Jane Blaffer Owen how to respond, "You just say, 'When you are in the arms of God, who needs arms?' "[32]

While describing the overall spirit of the *Pietà* as one of metamorphosis and transcendence, De Staebler stresses that such a transformation is not away from the earth but consistently informed by it.

> The forms that seem to be growing upward can be seen as flames as well as wings. They are still

ultimately earth forms. They are not ethereal
feathers of a bird. They are the stuff of the earth
that has power to transcend.[33]

The setting of the sculpture emphasizes its connection to
nature. The *Pietà* is placed in the northwest corner of Philip
Johnson's Roofless Church (1960: New Harmony, Indiana)
among three golden rain trees. De Staebler noted that he
had seen the fall coloring of those trees "with the most
beautiful burning golden leaf; and this sculpture I think will
be . . . like the fourth tree."[34]

Initially he had conceived of fusion of the two figures as
in the *Rondanini Pietà* "where you feel that Christ is connected to the torso of his mother, but frontally."[35] He
worked through a number of variations toward a more
simplified expression which became the sharing of one
torso on only two legs so that the fusion of two persons is
clear.

When you see it in the flesh like we are here, this
fusion . . . is very apparent. It does not read all
that well in a photograph; but when you see it in
the flesh . . . you can in your mind hold the
reality of two persons in one.[36]

While there are vestiges of separateness, such as the
head of Christ, that head emerges at the breast reminding
the viewer that Christ's body emerged from his mother's
and that, as a child, he was dependent on her for nourish-
ment. Theologically, one may think of Mary as a symbol of
the church and the church as the body of Christ.

Similarly, the two legs may be identified as reflecting

differences in the two persons; but the hole in each foot emphasizes the empathy of the mother for the son. De Staebler elaborated how the legs stress the difference of the two figures.

> I want to bring together a sense of great time and age with also a sense of youthfulness. The legs are functioning in two different ways. . . . This [right] leg is springing and youthful like a dancer. And this youthfulness carries right on up and fuses with the mother. But the son, who is younger chronologically, and who is dead and broken, is expressed by the left leg which is aging and weighted, rooted. So in the legs you get the simultaneous expression of dying and collapsing with rising and transcending. And it creates an ambiguousness, an encompassing sense of the opposites of death and transfiguration. To feel the body weighted on the body's left side, which is Christ's side, but lifting and pulling with strength on the other's side is the tension that is in the piece as I see it.[37]

The left leg did not show signs of rigor mortis in its joints; and De Staebler agreed "There is still strength. There is strength in death. But I meant for the character of the legs to be contrasting."[38] The holes in both feet expressed empathy and oneness in Christ, not only the unity of Christ and Mary but also the potential oneness of humanity and divinity.

> That is to express the empathy that Mary has been crucified as we all are who become empathetically

one with Christ. So there is no distinction as to
whose body was actually crucified. And the same
goes for the wound that appears on the mother's
side. That is an important symbolic key to the
overriding emotion of empathy. If you feel something totally, you are the other person as well.[39]

Such empathy and oneness with Christ were reflected in
the stigmata associated with St. Francis, the subject of De
Staebler's undergraduate thesis.

Attention to the two heads in the sculpture led De
Staebler to point out how nimbus shapes near the heads
relate them to each other and to the energy of the spirit.
Behind and around the head of Christ where it emerges
from the mother's body is one nimbus shape; and above the
mother's head, another is signified by "the wing [which] is a
nimbus in quality."[40] The iconography of the halo in Christianity interests De Staebler as a visual symbol for spiritual
energy. For him, "the radiation of energy from the spirit is
what the halo is all about."[41] A variation of the nimbus is
the mandorla. This larger oval-shaped area has been used
historically to enclose the resurrected Christ figure in majesty; but De Staebler incorporates the mandorla through
minimal form in his work.

The halo that fascinates me is the mandorla of the
tympana of the cathedrals where Christ sits inside
the form. The encompassing oval holds the Christ
in majesty. This sculpture is taking off from that.
It is not going the whole route, as an earlier
version would have expressed more of that encompassing aura. It is one thing to do it in relief as in
tympana of cathedrals; but to do it in space is

another matter entirely because then what you want to be immaterial becomes very material. Reducing that sense of the aura to a minimal form . . . is the only way I could deal with that.[42]

Color draws the viewer's attention upward toward those heads and mandorlas as gold tones, historically associated with halos, become prominent. De Staebler details the transition of colors and its effects.

The sheen of the bronze itself I brought out more and more as we go up from the feet. The tonality is most opaque at the ground. It has a whitish green opacity to it; and as you move upward, this slowly gives way to rich tones which are subdued and which I hope feel as though they are within, working outward and upward as you get to the head of Christ and then to the mother and then to the nimbus. The sense of inner light in the bronze itself is accentuated.[43]

The nimbus shapes and the golden color contribute to a sense of resurrection.

Interpretation of De Staebler's *Pietà* is aided by his own comments comparing and contrasting his work and Michelangelo's work. He responded most strongly to the *Rondanini Pietà* and particularly remembered the fusion of the torsos.[44] De Staebler cites approvingly Michelangelo's rejection of his earlier idealization of Christ's figure and his reworking the piece.

I think there is enough evidence to show that he was literally repelled by his neo-Platonic idealiza-

tion of Christ's figure. We know from the scale of
the original right arm of Christ left dangling that
he knocked the head off the first version and then
proceeded to carve anew the heads and bodies of
mother and son from the stone that remained
from the torso. My starting point was similarly to
place the Christ torso in front of the Mary torso.[45]

De Staebler was not satisfied with Michelangelo's arrangement of the two torsos, that is, the two individualized
forms placed one in front of the other; for such mass contributes to weightiness. By more completely merging the
two bodies into one, De Staebler achieves a sense of ascension.

What slowly emerged was the most economical
symbolic expression of empathy through fusion I
could arrive at. By making the fusion bisym-
metrical from the front rather than from front to
back, I was able to narrow the mass of the torsos
and therefore establish a sense of ascending which
would not have been possible if the center of
gravity had been held lower. Michelangelo's
Christ is completely in slump. The legs are buck-
led and he is held in a very tentative way by the
mother. He sketched in arms which are not
clearly defined. But the force of the sculpture is
still transcendent. Even though there is the col-
lapse of death, there is still the sense that death is
merely the way to another state. All that has been
very important in my own feelings about this
piece.[46]

Both the *Rondanini Pietà* and the New Harmony *Pietà* have a sense of human endurance which De Staebler attributes to the prominence of the torsos. Asked about the significance of the torso in his works, he recounted the importance of viewing the great torso of the *Belvedere Hercules* in the Vatican collection.

> I saw it when I was nineteen years old. I went to the recent Vatican touring exhibition almost solely to see it again. It is this magnificent twisting torso with no head, no arms, no legs. It just sits there, this gigantic statement of man's endurance. I think the Renaissance saw the formal purity in the truncated figure, which in time became a convention.[47]

While both sculptors gave significant focus to the torso and so communicated the human capacity for endurance, De Staebler's narrowing of the torso reduced the mass and contributed to a sense of ascension.

Whereas Michelangelo's frontal torso of Christ collapsed back into the mother, De Staebler's combined torsos thrust forward. He cited the imagery of dance when asked to discuss the sense of ascension impressed on the viewer by the torso thrusting forward. The forward thrust throws the figure off balance so that it would fall except for the nimbus or wing shape which seems to draw the figures up. He identified such symbolism with salvation.

> There is an ambivalence between collapse and ascension. All movement in dance is an illusion because the dancer is a split second away from

falling at each moment. But due to the methods you have identified here, the counter balance of the wing form, as an arm held by a dancer in a certain way, gives the illusion that the figure is for an instantaneous moment defying gravity. . . . Symbolically that is salvation. In spiritual terms you do not die with the body. The body is returning to its lowest common denominator through gravity, but the spirit floats free.[48]

The head of Christ contributes to the experience of birth as well as death. In this baldness as found in his *Crucifix*, Stephen De Staebler suggests the similarity between the newborn child and the aged old man.

Christ can be looked at as quite embryonic, almost fetal, almost emerging at that stage of pre-development. Certainly the skull, like a baby's skull born without any appreciable hair, has that feeling. It is a wonderful tie in with old age. You are born bald and you leave bald, if you live that long.[49]

De Staebler's *Pietà* thus signifies both birth and death.

Jane Blaffer Owen reports her understanding of this simultaneous experience of birth, death, and resurrection with the New Harmony *Pietà*.

De Staebler believes, like St. Paul before him, that death does not separate us from life or the love of God. Ascent and descent were staples of his vocabulary whenever we spoke of his hopes for this ambitious endeavor. Gradually, the rising and falling of fountains, the crests and valleys of ocean waves, paths up a mountain and paths down became part of my thinking, too. I began to imagine that a mountain itself stood for my imperishable soul, and that life and death were two sides of one reality; the mountain remaining the same. But this was thinking and feeling for me, not seeing. And however often one might read St. Paul, or repeat the affirmations of the Nicean Creed, do we, as often, usually see life proceeding from death and hope rising from tragedy?

Let us take a look at another Pietà, Michelangelo's last, and perhaps greatest work, the *Rondanini Pietà*. The dead Christ and his mother are hewn from a single block of marble and conceived vertically. Mary does not bend under her sorrow, but supports her son. . . . Michelangelo, however, does not unify the two figures; and he does not promise us a resurrection, as does the De Staebler *Pietà*. Here the bowed head of Christ emerging from his mother's side is as much of a newborn infant as it is the head of one who has died. The stripes on his back, the pierced feet, and broken thigh tell us a crucifixion has taken place. Mary is also gravely wounded, for are not mother and child flesh and bone of one another? But Christ is no longer the suffering servant; and his mother's agony is behind her. The eyes look ahead, not down, the lips are firm, and she strides forward with lilting steps. The flames like a banner above her head, tattered though it may be,

13. Stephen De Staebler, *Standing Man and Woman*, 1975. Fired clay.
96 × 33 × 33 inches. Private Collection. Photograph by Susan Felter.
Courtesy Stephen De Staebler.

link her humanity with the source of all life. Grief is not embraced, retained, or glorified; and tragedy is transcended.

These are large thoughts, but they can speak directly to us in New Harmony, and to visitors in this court. Not long ago a woman I did not know burst into tears when she saw our *Pietà*. She had little, if any, experience of art, but she told me the story of the recent loss of a son. Then I spoke of the death of my daughter Carol. Two strangers grew very close in that moment, and closer to the Mother of God than either of them had been before.[50]

Art critic Thomas Albright described De Staebler's early works, such as *Standing Man and Standing Woman* (1975: Private Collection) (fig. 13), as "contemporary parables of death and resurrection."[51] In those earlier works, there is a tension between what is and what is yet to come. Jane Dillenberger noted, "In tension, there is action. De Staebler's sculptures do not repose. Instead they yearn. One might say that will is at war with being."[52] In that tension, action, and yearning, the sculptures present a communitive experience of transcendence through the human body. Throughout his work, the combination of incompletion and submerged order create a persistence of individual personality that endures even as the body gives way to other less specifiable forms, such as in *Archangel* or *Pietà*. Stephen De Staebler's art offers a vision of graceful aging, dying, and rising.

3

Jasper Johns's Paintings:
Postcritical Philosophies

*A*rt critic Jill Johnston enumerated many instances in which Jasper Johns's works of art
included symbols of crucifixion and resurrection primarily
from Mathias Grünewald's *Isenheim Altarpiece* (1515: Musée d'Unterlinden, Colmar).[1] Reviewing such evidence
within a larger context of his work reveals that Johns's
concerns are more epistemological than iconographic. In
the light of his concerns, one learns not to interpret iconographic details in terms of their use in earlier art by others
or by Johns himself. In his work, resurrection relates to
realizing the possibility of knowing rather than to any particular knowledge; and crucifixion to falling short of that
realization. Johns's primary significance for religious studies
stems from connections of his work to postcritical philosophies.

Jasper Johns has overcome the abstract-expressionist/
pop-art dichotomy in art just as Michael Polanyi overcame
the subjective/objective and the mind/body dichotomies in
epistemology. Succumbing to these dichotomies crucifies
one's quest for knowing. Overcoming these dichotomies
resurrects such quests. Johns explicitly drew on Ludwig
Wittgenstein's later work. Hence his art is particularly fruit-

ful for exploring the ramifications of Wittgenstein's emphasis on meaning as a function of use in context. Indwelling Johns's art enables us to recognize many parallels among the insights of Johns, Polanyi, and Wittgenstein that make one aware of human bodies in the process of knowing. Jasper Johns's works are particularly suited to this purpose, for they are designed to make us aware of all that we *bring to* a viewing of art, much of which either prevents us from seeing or enables us to see.

Johns creates works of beauty. Part of his genius lies in creating works which are as beautiful as anything in abstract expressionism and indeed seem like such expressionism in the sensuous effects of the paint and color. His art is also as mundane in subject matter and as in touch with concrete reality as the pop art with which his work bears affinities. After seeing Johns's works, a friend commented how she was reminded of Paul Cézanne's paintings. This is a most insightful remark because it may be argued that Johns stands in relation to the art before and after him in the twentieth century much as Cézanne did to that before and after him in the nineteenth century. Both artists were concerned with promoting particular ways of looking at the world, and with painting that took seriously human relationship to the world. That relationship, at times ambiguous and fraught with difficulties, was nonetheless affirmed in their art. Both men accepted the world and human placement within it as concerns which may be explored in painting without slipping into either "objective realism" or "subjective solipsism"; that is, without slipping into either representational art and pop art on the one hand, or impressionism and abstract expressionism on the other hand. Thus, that laughter should have at times been the reaction to both men's works is appropriate. The works of both artists appear absurd to a public that cannot imagine treating the world of concrete reality, apples in the case of Cézanne or ale cans in the case of Johns, with such care and seriousness, and which cannot affirm the relationship of such seemingly disjunctive entities as mind and body.

An initial reaction to a survey of Johns's works is "He keeps doing the same things." In reality, they are never the same. There is always a significant difference in color, size, background, or media. An initial look at Johns's art is an important confessional experience for one interested in art who might otherwise not realize, or never admit to oneself much less to others, how little one actually observes. The first lesson to be learned from taking a second look at Johns's paintings and lithographs is the many ways in which one unwittingly brings a critical optical and mental apparatus to the "viewing" of paintings, an apparatus which prevents seeing what is really presented in the art.

Consider *Sketch for The Critic Sees* (1961: Collection of Leo Castelli) (fig. 24). If one attends to Johns's work, one sees not eyes but mouths behind the glasses. A casual first glance might miss the presence of these mouths where eyes should be; but a closer look at the sculpture and at Johns's drawing for the work reveals this ominous yet humorous presence. Max Kozloff has written that the

> critic is blinded from seeing by his own words. . . . We see not with our eyes but through the concepts we bring to a particular situation. . . . We tend to obliterate those facts which contradict that which we already know and anticipate.[2]

Judith Stein sees this sculpture as a warning that the art

world and its patrons consume and do not see art.[3] A philosophical parallel is Wittgenstein's oft-repeated admonition against philosophical blinders, "Don't think; look!" Wittgenstein noted that one's previous education could blind one to new insights:

> One cannot guess how a word functions. One has to *look at* its use and learn from that. But the difficulty is to remove the prejudice which stands in the way of doing this. It is not a *stupid* prejudice.[4]

While these interpretations fall within Johns's concerns, another word needs to be added to restore the ambiguity of *Sketch for the Critic Sees*. Johns's interest in Marshall McLuhan's thought lends itself to a positive interpretation, while not denying the negative ones. McLuhan concluded that it is the eye and its isolated overemphasis in the critical sensorium that leads to the analytical disposition of modern humanity to dissect life into dichotomous parts. To McLuhan the mouth as well as the ear, the sense of taste as well as hearing, helped to correct the detached, overly analytical approach of the eye. Thus they bring to the experiencing of life and art a highly participatory dimension which avoids the subject/object dichotomy. There can be no ultimate dichotomy between subject and object when one eats the other.

At a deeper level it has been argued by Michael Polanyi that the subject/object dichotomy is a philosophical bogeyman created by modern humanity's demand for complete precision and objective certainty. Polanyi made it abundantly clear that all knowledge is at base tacit in char-

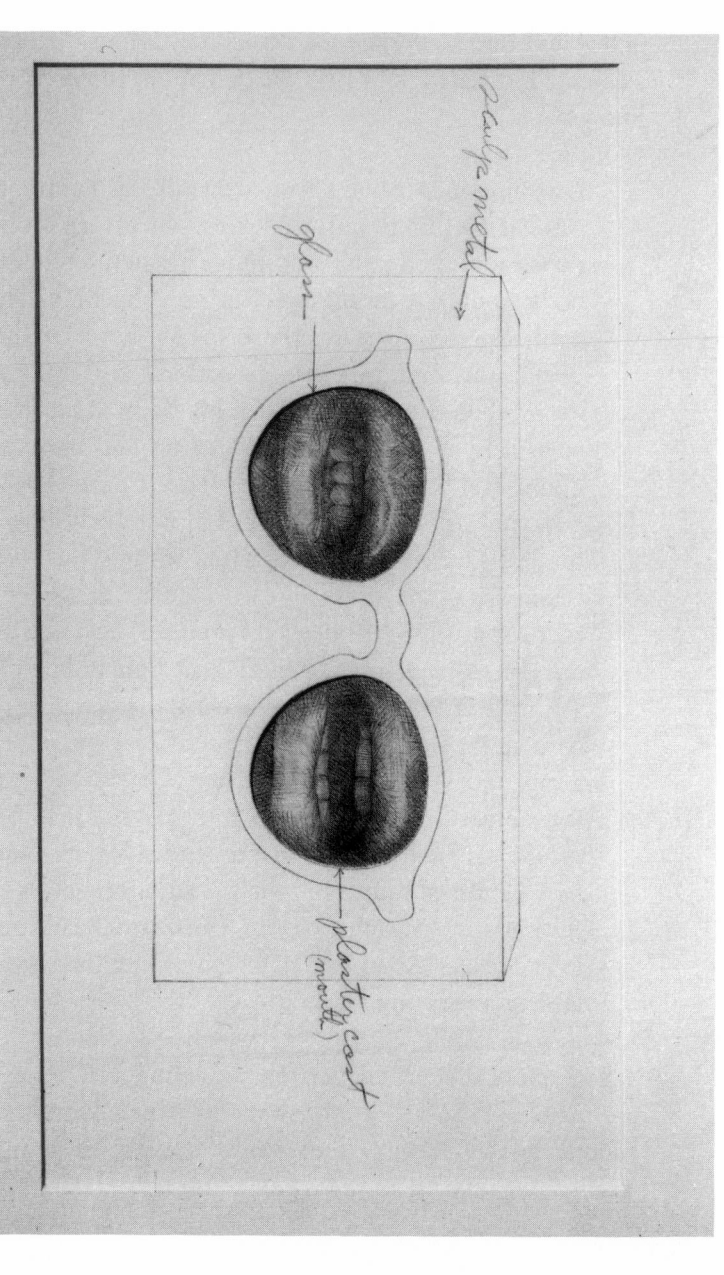

24. Jasper Johns, *Sketch for the Critic Sees*, 1962. Pencil and collage on paper. 10½ × 14¼ inches. Signed LR: The Critic Sees, J. Johns, '62. Collection Leo Castelli, New York. Photograph by Jim Strong. Courtesy Jasper Johns, LC #157. © Jasper Johns/VAGA, New York 1991.

acter, and that tacit knowing arises only when the knowing subject "indwells," by active participation, the reality to be known.

> Dwelling in our body clearly enables us to attend *from* it to things outside, while an external observer will tend to look *at* things happening in the body, seeing it as an object or as a machine. He will miss the meaning these events have for the person dwelling in the body and fail to share the experience the person has of his body. Again we have loss of meaning by alienation and another glimpse of the meaning of dualism. I have shown how our subsidiary awareness of our body is extended to include a stick, when we feel our way by means of the stick. To use language in speech, reading and writing, is to extend our bodily equipment and become intelligent human beings. We may say that when we learn to use language, or a probe, or a tool, and thus make ourselves aware of these things as we are of our body, we *interiorize* these things and *make ourselves dwell in them.* Such extensions of ourselves develop new faculties in us; our whole education operates in this way; as each of us interiorizes our cultural heritage, he grows into a person seeing the world and experiencing life in terms of this outlook.[5]

The contradictory suggestions of eating and being eaten are present in many of Johns's works which offer forks and spoons to the viewer. Such works are not as straightforwardly negative or ominous as some critics suppose. Although Johns is concerned with being "eaten up" by critics without appreciation, he does not object to offering himself up in this "eating-being-eaten process" where it leads to growth. That one should be aware of *what* and *how* one is eating is Johns's concern. The viewer is the critic as *Sketch for the Critic Smiles* (1959: Collection of the Artist) helps one realize. Richard Field has noted, "The critic smiles only when we realize the pun implied by the substitution of the crowned teeth for bristles [in the sculpted toothbrush]. But it is we who smile!"[6] The title of the work of art then derives from the interaction of the viewer with the painting or sculpture, and not from the painting or sculpture alone. "It is our awareness that Johns has made us behave by smiling that is the real experience."[7] Thus paintings or sculptures are not subjects for Johns. As Field noted:

> Doubtlessly both Johns's daring and frustration spring from his willingness to strip art of its sub-ject-content dichotomy in order to concentrate on the questions of how we respond to that undefin-able part of civilization we call art.[8]

Thus the "meaning" of the sculpture is a mediated syn-thesis of the work, its title, and viewer's response. It is understood in the same way that a joke is understood. Art, like language, is not an inert object for passive observation. It is, rather, a tool or activity for affecting people. Meaning is not "read-off" by, or squeezed out of, an antiseptic analy-sis of the constituent parts, as the logical atomists and positivists would have us believe. It is, according to Witt-genstein, a function of human activity within concrete con-texts for social purposes.

> But how many kinds of sentences are there? Say
> assertion, question, and command?—There are
> *countless* kinds: countless different kinds of use of
> what we call "symbols," "words," "sentences."
> And this multiplicity is not something fixed, given
> once for all; but new types of language, new lan-
> guage-games, as we may say, come into existence,
> and others become obsolete and get forgotten.
> (We can get a *rough picture* of this from the
> changes in mathematics.) Here the term "lan-
> guage *game*" is meant to bring into prominence
> the fact that the *speaking* of language is part of an
> activity, or of a form of life.[9]

Leo Steinberg's negative, ominous judgment that Johns's
works convey a sense of desolate waiting[10] can be seen as
the reverse side of Solomon's more optimistic appraisal that
Johns's works invite the participation and indeed demand
the presence of viewers.[11] In looking at the *Fool's House*
(1962: Private Collection) (fig. 25), one is tempted to reach
out for the coffee cup, the broom, or the rag. In noting this,
one may laugh. Only later one may observe that the title
Fool's House, as it appears in the painting, may also be read
"Use Fool's Ho." Thus one knows oneself to be a fool who
by laughter comes to *see* relationship with the art.

Johns purposely chooses "subjects" that are, as Steinberg
summarizes, commonplace, of conventional shape, flat,
systems unto themselves, neutral, muted, and "man-
made."[12] By choosing common items, Johns takes advan-
tage of the viewer's initial tendency to treat such subjects
with only a passing glance. The grey color or limited palate
of many of his works is likewise selected so as not to make

25. Jasper Johns, *Fool's House*, 1962. Oil on canvas with objects. 72 × 36 inches. Private Collection, New York. Photograph by Rudolph Burckhardt. Courtesy Jasper Johns, LC #155. © Jasper Johns/VAGA, New York 1991.

too explicit the many subtle differences in the works. Johns purposely treats the "same" subject in different media so as to introduce additional subtle differences. His "coat-hanger paintings" are rendered in both paint and lithograph. Field notes some differences between *Coat Hanger I* (1960: published by ULAE, Private Collection) as a lithograph and the original Johns's work:

> Coat Hanger I . . . includes at the upper right some horizontal lines that derive from those in the original drawing (at the upper left). . . . The sense that this work is different from any other coat hanger executed by Johns will not be felt by those whose attention is riveted on the "subject."[13]

Literally deeper distinctions appear in paintings of the same subject but where different collages from newspapers and books are underneath the paint. In the flag paintings, beneath the stripes of one there is a photograph of a face; but beneath the stripes of others, one discovers articles about Billy Graham preaching at the White House and other current events. In one of the map paintings, *Map* (1962: Private Collection), one finds under Idaho a page from Albert Camus's novel, *The Rebel*; and under Kansas, one finds a newspaper column on wheat prices.

In emphasizing the overlooked, common items, Johns, of course, chooses to paint or sculpt Ballantine Ale cans because they are, as the label clearly reads, "America's largest selling ale." John Cage told of Johns's interchange with one lady at the opening featuring the *Painted Bronze* (1960: Neue Galerie, Aachen).

Another lady, outraged by the beer cans that were exhibited in the gallery said, "What are they doing here?" Then Johns explained that they were not beer cans but had taken him much time and effort to make, that if she examined them closely she would notice among other things fingerprints, that moreover she might also observe that they were not the same height (i.e., had not come off an assembly line.) Why, he asks, was she won over? Why does the information that someone has done something affect the judgment of another? Why cannot someone who is looking at something do his own work of looking?[14]

Solomon reported how Johns was inspired to create this work. The idea came to Johns from Wilhem de Kooning's comment about Johns's art dealer, "Give that Leo Castelli two beer cans and he could sell them!"[15] Viewers may think they are identical, but they are not. One is empty with holes in the top. The other is without holes and appears full. One has a plain top like the cans that come from New York. The other has three rings on top like the cans that come from Florida. As Johns told the woman, one can was made smaller than the other.

This preference for the common, ordinary dimension of experience represents yet another similarity between Johns and Wittgenstein. The latter constantly reminded philosophers who had lost their way in the labyrinth of language, who had become trapped in the fly-bottle, that the way out does not lie in the direction of abstraction and/or logical analysis. It lies, rather, in regaining a familiarity with common, ordinary language as it is spoken in the everyday world. Such language already contains a vast number of subtle distinctions and shades of meaning to which attention only needs to be paid. Appropriately enough, Wittgenstein considered using as the epigram for *Philosophical Investigations* what Kent told Lear, "I'll teach you differences."[16] Concerning the contrast between logical analysis and ordinary speech, Wittgenstein gave this poignant metaphor.

> The more narrowly we examine actual language, the sharper becomes the conflict between it and our requirement. (For the crystalline purity of logic was, of course, not a *result of investigation*: it was a requirement.) The conflict becomes intolerable; the requirement is now in danger of becoming empty. We have got on to slippery ice where there is no friction and so in a certain sense the conditions are ideal, but also, just because of that, we are unable to walk. We want to walk: so we need *friction*. Back to the rough ground![17]

Solomon summarized Johns's program in art which resonated with Wittgenstein's program in philosophy. Johns uses very plain subject matter but always communicates something different. We are forced to commit more of our attention than usual to see the infinite variation in such ordinary experiences. In a world pressed toward reduction of all meaning to standardized parts, "Jasper Johns opens a door on intuition, on ambiguity, and on an unconfined realm of human feeling."[18]

These references to commitment, intuition, and feeling have a clear Polanyian ring. Throughout his works, Polanyi sought to underline the necessity of what he termed "the

personal coefficient" in all knowing. To affirm a proposition
is to claim a discovery and to commit oneself to it. Moreover, such an affirmation entails a commitment to a know-
able reality and the actuality of knowing it. Likewise, in all
his works Polanyi sought to establish the epistemological
priority of tacit knowing (an integrative, intuitive act),
based in subsidiary awareness and embodied activity (in-
volving values and feelings).

> The arts of doing and knowing, the valuation and
> the understanding of meanings, are thus seen to
> be only different aspects of the act of extending
> our person into the subsidiary awareness of par-
> ticulars which compose a whole. The inherent
> structure of this fundamental act of personal
> knowing makes us both necessarily participate in
> its shaping and acknowledge its results with uni-
> versal intent. This is the prototype of intellectual
> commitment.
>
> It is the act of commitment in its full structure
> that saves personal knowledge from being merely
> subjective. Intellectual commitment is a responsi-
> ble decision, in submission to the compelling
> claims of what in good conscience I conceive to be
> true. It is an act of hope, striving to fulfill an
> obligation within a personal situation for which I
> am not responsible and which therefore deter-
> mines my calling. This hope and this obligation
> are expressed in the universal intent of personal
> knowledge.[19]

In Polanyi's epistemology, Wittgentein's language analysis, and Johns's painting, bodies of knowledge are revealed

to be dependent literally on the bodies of the knowers and the worlds they indwell. The meaning of a word cannot be known without a knowledge of the person using it and the context in which it is used. Likewise, meaningful discussion about a painting requires attention to the wider worlds which the artist and viewer indwell. Such attention may be tacit or explicit; but one must be careful not to assume a uniformity of subject matter and so overlook the context which governs its meaning.

Johns's paintings require careful attention to the context. Examination of the works titled *No* (1961: Collection of the Artist) (fig. 26) clarifies Johns's intentions. If one is asked, "What do you see?" one is likely to respond, "There is a canvas with a bit of wire dangling down it, with the word *No* attached to the end of the wire and casting a shadow on the canvas." The very word *No* warns one against this initial view, based as it is on one's memory of how light, shadow, and perspective operate. In reality, the NO is glued to the paper, but appears to be attached to the embossed wire and hanging free! The shadow is painted on the canvas.

In many ways the word *No* seems to caution the observer against jumping to conclusions about the nature of what is being seen.[20] Johns's fondness for Japan suggests other meanings as well. In Noh Theater, "Noh time, protracted gesture, and speech in contrast to content" make a "high demand on audience projection."[21]

Johns's intentions are only partially seen by concluding with the pop artists that "one has to look anew at everything." Johns rejects the appellation "father of pop art." Pop art continues the human's role in the world as observer. Johns pushes viewers to recognize and fulfill their roles as namers, creators, and agents in the ongoing process of art

26. Jasper Johns, *No*, 1961. Encaustic, collage, and sculptmetal on canvas with objects. 68 × 40 inches. Collection of the Artist. Photograph by Rudolph Burckhardt. Courtesy Jasper Johns, LC #111. © Jasper Johns/VAGA, New York 1991.

and the world. Johns himself described this more demand-
ing role.

> There is a great deal of intention in painting; it's
> rather unavoidable. But when a work is let out by
> the artist and said to be complete, the intention
> loosens. Then it's subject to all kinds of use and
> misuse and pun. Occasionally someone will see
> the work in a way that even changes its signifi-
> cance for the person who made it; the work is no
> longer "intention," but the thing being seen and
> someone responding to it. They will see it in a
> way that makes you think, that is a possible way of
> seeing it. Then you, as the artist, can enjoy it—
> that's possible—or you can lament it. If you like,
> you can try to express the intention more clearly
> in another work. But what is interesting is anyone
> having the experience he has![22]

The viewer and the artist are parts of the context in
which a painting has its life. Both contribute to its meaning.
Therefore, the connections which the viewers and the artists have to the cultures which they indwell must be considered. Changing meanings are understandable as a result of
such complex indwelling and interaction. Johns noted his
own delight in such change:

> There seems to be a sort of "pressure area" "un-
> derneath" language which operates in such a way
> as to force the language to change. (I'm believing
> painting to be a language, or wishing language to
> be any sort of recognition.) If one takes delight in

that kind of changing process one moves toward new recognitions, names, images.[23]

Here Johns would seem to be working with Wittgenstein's notion of language as "open-textured." Wittgenstein conceived of language as a living organism, with new expressions and language-games evolving and others dropping out of use.

> Ask yourself whether our language is complete; whether it was so before the symbolism of chemistry and the notation of the infinitesimal calculus were incorporated in it; for these are, so to speak, suburbs of our language. (And how many houses or streets does it take before a town begins to be a town?) Our language can be seen as an ancient city: a maze of little streets and squares, of old and new houses, and of houses with additions from various periods; and this surrounded by a multitude of new boroughs with straight and regular streets and uniform houses.[24]

For Johns, the problem is that the viewer is like a watchman who is not conscious of what he brings to a place and therefore takes away very little or nothing. Thus he contributes neither to change in himself nor in others. Viewers are the watchmen when approaching a work of art not realizing that the memories and expectations they possess easily destroy an art experience; and so, they take away no new awareness which would change them or the world. Viewers need to be more like the spy who is very cognizant of what he brings to a place and of what he finds there; so, he will not leave what he brings or disturb what he finds in ways that will give him away or mislead him as to what was there. The spy then does take away new insights which do change him and the world.

In *Good Time Charley* (1961: Private Collection) the stick moves and even the "same" work of art has the capacity to change if the viewers interact with it. The measuring stick, which is usually used in creating something, can destroy part of the paintings as in *Good Time Charley*. What happens when we approach a work of art with preconceived measuring sticks as to how certain space and objects should be handled? Such preconceptions prevent the "same" object from taking on different uses and meanings in other paintings or even in the same painting. Solomon stresses that Johns's works avoid specific meanings and keep the images ambiguous. By such ambiguity, he questions "established values in order to arrive at newer and richer values, and it is in precisely this sense that Johns represents a major departure for a whole new generation of artists."[25]

In looking at Johns's *Three Flags* (1958: The Whitney Museum of American Art, New York), one needs to listen to Richard Field's advice more now than at the time the painting was created before the Vietnam War:

> The richly variegated and marvelous satisfactions of a Johns's work are the more apprehended the more one is capable of suspended judgment, of tolerating ambiguity and uncertainty, of surviving an impure situation which interweaves a variety of modes of perception and knowledge.[26]

Johns reported that he simply dreamed one night of painting a large flag. Most of his flags strike the viewer as looking as they should—as looking right. The fact that one finds the flag congenial in appearance is what John Cage calls a "paradox in broad daylight"—proof that asymmetry is symmetry.[27] One is so accustomed to the flag's proportions that one does not realize its radical asymmetry. In the days of forty-eight states, Cage noted the similarity of the American flag to the sonnet; the division of the fourteen lines into eight and six in such poetry and in the field of stars. To obscure and clarify this division is a concern of poetry and Johns's painting alike.

As the flags stress the role of our memories in judging works as symmetrical, Johns's beautiful painted numerals, such as *Figure 5* (1955: Private Collection), recall the bodily root of the decimal system. The body is more explicitly present in Johns's casts of human body parts in paintings such as *Target With Four Faces* (1955: The Museum of Modern Art, New York) and *Target With Plaster Casts* (1955: Private Collection). In those early works and in many Johns's lithographs, the body parts are separated from one another. In his recent series, *Seasons*, Johns presents the shadow of his own complete body.

Even in his early works, one is led to see the participation of our human form in relating to all art. His naming of one of these works *Out The Window* (1959: Private Collection) stresses ironically the way in which Johns reveals the relation of human form not only to art but to the rest of the world as well.

> Johns's sister visited the studio and found no meaning in the "emptiness" of the picture; she looked out at the vacant parking lot across the street, and remarked that he seemed to paint what he saw out his window.[28]

Language analysis in the later work of Wittgenstein stresses the use and user of words. The word itself or even the sentence cannot make plain its meaning: Is it to be taken seriously or ironically? Is the user telling the truth or lying? Johns makes one aware of similar problems in art that force one to take a second look and think about a series of works. In *Painting With Two Balls* (1960: Collection of the Artist), one is reasonably certain that the two balls are used to keep the two canvases apart so that one sees through them and to the wall. But in the lithograph of the same title, what is the function of the balls? At least one of their uses has changed. Johns discusses how his works reveal such change.

> This whole idea that anything can be one thing is an idea that interests me. I like the idea of taking discrete operations and using them in such a way that casts doubt upon them and one is not sure what to regard as a discrete thing.[29]

In *Device Circle* (1959: Private Collection), many of one's perceptions are called into question with typical Johnsian delight. Here his use of light and dark values invert the conventions of painting. His use of irony contradicts what one supposes to be the case: the flat letters are painted to look three-dimensional and the three-dimensional stick appears to be flat with the painting's surface.[30]

Johns's ironical *Device Circle* also suggests Leonardo's work in which the human figure is the measure of all things: *The Proportions of the Human Figure, after Vitruvius* (1492: Academy, Venice) (fig. 27). Johns would subscribe to the role of humans as measures and measurers of all things.

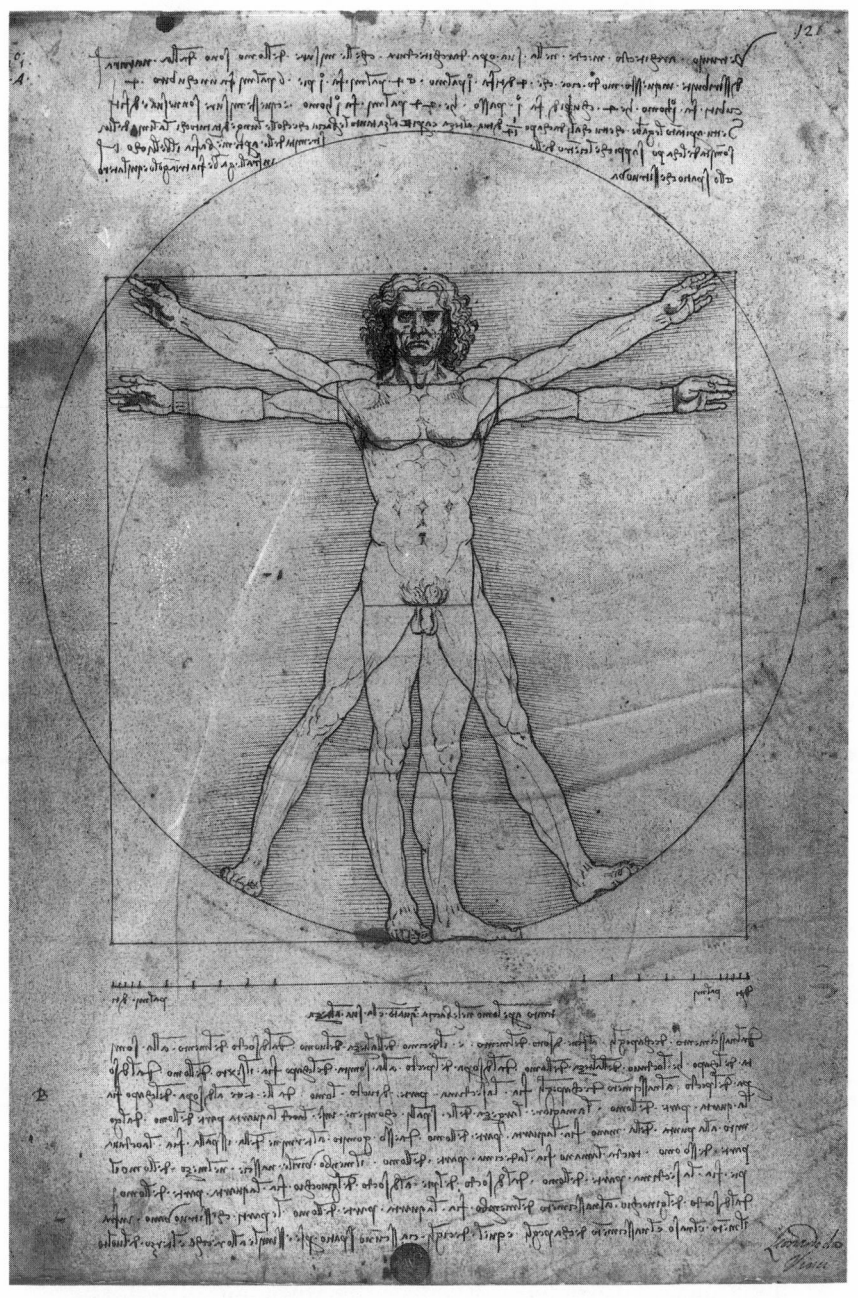

27. Leonardo da Vinci, *The Proportions of the Human Figure after Vitruvius*, c. 1492. Academy, Venice. Courtesy of Alinari/Art Resource, New York.

He would only caution viewers to realize consciously that they are applying to works of art the standards that they bring with them. In his series *Seasons*, Johns extends that inquiry. An arm replaces the measuring stick as the measure of all things as it did in his earlier work, *Periscope (Hart Crane)* (1963: Collection of the Artist) (fig. 28).

In three works of 1963, *Periscope (Hart Crane)*, *Hatteras*, (1963: Private Collection), and *Land's End*, (1963: San Francisco Museum of Modern Art) (fig. 29), Johns comes most closely to revealing the destructive and creative forces of humans measuring art. These paintings relate to Hart Crane's poem, "Cape Hatteras," from which Johns's work *Periscope (Hart Crane)* receives its name.

> *The captured fume of space foams in our ears—*
> *What whisperings of far watches on the main*
> *Relapsing into silence, while time clears*
> *Our lenses, lifts a focus, resurrects*
> *A periscope to glimpse what joys or pain*
> *our eyes can share or answer then deflects*
> *Us, shunting to a labyrinth submersed*
> *Where each sees only his dim past reversed. . . .*[31]

When one consciously brings to the work of art an awareness of memories, striving to see the work of art anew in spite of what one expects, one may gain a glimpse of "joys or pain our eyes can share or answer," as we see in *Periscope (Hart Crane)* or *Hatteras*. When one loses awareness of all the expectations and measuring devices that one brings to the work of art and thinks instead that one may approach it "objectively," one is deflected and shunted "to a labyrinth submersed where each sees only his dim past reversed." Even in the reversing of letters,

28. Jasper Johns, *Periscope (Hart Crane)*, 1963. Oil on canvas. 67 × 48 inches. Collection of the Artist. Photograph by Rudolph Burckhardt. Courtesy Jasper Johns, LC #180. © Jasper Johns/VAGA, New York 1991.

one's expectations become clear as in *Land's End* where not all the letters have the counterparts one expects in a mirror image.

A helpful epistemological schema in understanding the main thrust of Johns's work is offered by Polanyi in his analysis of tacit knowing. Focal awareness and thus explicit knowledge of any entity is mediated out of our subsidiary awareness and thus the tacit knowledge of the particulars comprising it. One attends *to* the former *from* (or through) the latter. So one attends tacitly or subsidiarily to where one's fingers hold the hammer's handle as one attends explicitly or focally to where the hammer's head hits a nail. If one shifts explicit attention to where fingers hold the hammer, wielding of the hammer becomes clumsy; and one probably misses the nail. Similarly, explicit focus on one's fingers playing the piano usually destroys the performance. Explicit attention to the comprehensive entity constitutes the meaning of the particulars of which it is comprised. Positivism destroys meaning, for it would reverse the process and interpret meaning of higher comprehensive entities in terms of lower particulars by focusing explicitly on those particulars. Ideas are reduced to self-interest: economic, sexual, or survival in such reductionisms as Marxism, Freudianism, or Darwinism. Such focal attention to particulars is congenial to deconstruction, pathology, and Mark Taylor's a/theology. However, a reversal of attention is necessary for construction and theology. Polanyi details how the comprehensive entity (Gestalt) constitutes the meaning of the particulars of which it is comprised.

> When we are relying on our awareness of something (A) for attending to something else (B), we are but subsidiarily aware of A. The thing B, to

29. Jasper Johns, *Land's End*, 1963. Oil on canvas. 67 × 48 inches. San Francisco Museum of Modern Art. Gift of Mr. and Mrs. Harry W. Anderson. Photo Credit: Don Myer. © Jasper Johns/VAGA, New York 1991.

which we are thus focally attending, is then the meaning of A. The focal object B is always identifiable, while things like A, of which we are subsidiarily aware, may be unidentifiable. The two kinds of awareness are mutually exclusive: when we switch our attention to something of which we have hitherto been subsidiarily aware, it loses its previous meaning. Such is briefly *the structure of tacit knowing.*[32]

Similarly, Johns constantly adjusts, reverses, and ignores the particulars of what one sees in order (1) to call one's attention to the dynamics of the knowing (seeing) process itself; (2) to jar one into seeing things afresh; and (3) to stimulate one to interact with our environment in ways which will be creative in themselves. He interrupts one's conditioned "from-to" patterns in order to help one establish new patterns continually.

Johns's conception of the "spy" over against the "watchman" has already been introduced. In the renderings of the latter in a painting and in a lithograph, one sees something of the watchman's destructive force: *Watchman* (1964: Private Collection) (fig. 30). The areas of the canvas and paint are obliterated in the space beneath the watchman's chair. That the chair represents the functions of the critic (in at least one meaning) is reinforced by the fact that the body cast in the chair is that of the Japanese art critic Shuzo Takiguchi.[33] Furthermore, one may remember McLuhan's comment on chairs:

If the nineteenth century was the age of the editorial chair, the private point of view, ours is the

30. Jasper Johns, *Watchman*, 1964. Oil on canvas with objects. 85 × 60¼ inches. Private Collection, Japan. Photograph © Dorothy Zeidman. Courtesy Jasper Johns, LC #212. © Jasper Johns/VAGA, New York 1991.

century of the psychiatrist couch. As extension of
man, the chair is a specialist ablation of the pos-
terior, a sort of ablative absolute of the backside,
whereas the couch extends the integral being.[34]

The suggestion of destructiveness is further emphasized by
the action of the stick and ball below, and by the drippings
of paint throughout the painting below the chair. This
quasi-satire on the sexual self-assertion of "action painting"
shows the general damage done to a work of art by our
overlaying it with our own preconceptions.

Pinion (1963–64: Private Collection) contains further ambiguities which bear on the issue of the onlooker's relation
to the work of art. One meaning of "pinion" refers to a
"small cogwheel engaging with a larger cogwheel or with a
rack." This feature of engagement is analogous to one's
relation with an art work. A further meaning is the clipping
of the wings—a clipping that renders flight impossible; and
in this work, such a pinioning of the artist himself may be
seen. This action of pinioning the artist by the watchman in
each viewer prevents the artist from carrying out his task.

Johns is concerned with restoring to the viewer, as far as
possible, an experience of what is truly and potentially
present of one's expectations and memories in encounter-
ing the artwork. It is not that Johns wishes to deny memories and the expressionist ways of approaching life and art,
but he wishes also to make accessible the experiencing of
something new. *Pinion* warns the viewer of the danger of
losing contact with real objects by showing that one cannot
rely on the Platonic theory that would lull one into the
assumption that physical objects, while less "real" than
ideas, are more "real" than the "illusions" (copies) of art.

The area at the top of the painting is a two-dimensional photographic plate of Johns's previous work dealing with kitchen objects. The area in the lower section contains the actual three-dimensional object, a wire, and an actual two-dimensional painting. Yet one is more intrigued by the vague, two-dimensional photographic plate of an illusionary painting than by either the actual three-dimensional wire or the actual two-dimensional painting below. Field describes its dynamics as undermining the thought that a three-dimensional object is closer than a painting to the "idea." *Pinion* demonstrates the opposite as the object itself is far less evocative than the two-dimensional illusion of an object. "The illusion of an object is richer precisely because illusion is built upon memory and a priori expectations which the concrete tends to deny."[35]

An empty chair appears in *According to What* (1964: Private Collection). The title of the painting invites the alternative question "According to Whom?" The empty chair raises a similar question. There is destruction in the area of the canvas beneath the chair, in contrast to the vivid color and interesting areas in other parts of the canvas. Here is an object one has seen before, the hanger; but what is its use here? Many of Johns's "objects" appear again and again.

In *Field Painting* (1963–64: Private Collection), the Ballantine Ale can reappears, but in quite a new context so one is forced to reassess appraisal of it. In *Decoy* (1964: Private Collection) many of Johns's works reappear; but again one is left wondering about their new use. And if this is, in fact, a decoy, one suspects that oneself is the duck.

Johns's *Souvenir 2* (1964: Private Collection) comes closest to revealing the operations of his spy motif. One is here

forced in many ways to realize that one is a part of the work
of art and brings much to it. Johns himself looks at the
viewer from the dinner plate. One is invited to feast, but
with an awareness of what one brings to the work. A reversed canvas is superimposed on the main canvas so that
the viewers have a sense that someone is behind it looking
at them and painting them. What is he painting? What does
he see the viewers bringing to this painting, what memories or expectations of which they are unaware? They are
made aware that there is much present in them and in the
painting which they do not see. The bringing of memories
to the viewing of a work of art is not denied. One cannot
avoid the role memories play in viewing art; indeed it is the
only way one can see at all. The more one is aware of this
fact, the more one will actually see and experience in art.
Spies see more than watchmen.

In several of Johns's more recent works, he continues to
use the human body to explore epistemological issues
which he had dealt with earlier through the motifs of the
watchman and the spy. In these recent works, crucifixion
and resurrection have been recognized as significant motifs.
Jill Johnston noted the outline of a soldier from Grünewald's
resurrection panel in at least three of Johns's works such as
Untitled (1983: Collection of the Artist). She saw the outline
of a human body from Grünewald's St. Anthony panel in at
least nine Johns paintings. The inverted leg of that figure
appears in his *Fall* from the *Seasons*.[36] In each panel of that
series, *Spring* (1986: Private Collection), *Summer* (1985:
Private Collection), *Fall* (1986: Collection of the Artist), and
Winter (1986: Private Collection), one sees what Barbara
Rose called "pinioned palms,"[37] which Jill Johnston charac-
terized as "inescapably resembling stigmata."[38] Such refer-

ences would connect the works to the wounds in Jesus's hands produced by the crucifixion and evident in resurrection. First appearing in his *Periscope (Hart Crane)* and *Land's End*, the pinioned palms and other imagery of crucifixion and resurrection are not new in Johns's work, but are newly recognized.

The epistemological concern of the crucifixion motif is evidenced in the *Fall* (fig. 31). Mark Rosenthal noted "the partial figures signify the split between the realms of thought and feeling."[39] The body is split as the head with the right side of the body is separated by the central part of the painting from the left side of the body. The mind/body dichotomy is explicit. Other signs which may be associated with crucifixion or death are presented in the center of the painting: the broken ladder, the skull, and the cups and jar which are tipped over below the hand with the stigmata. A rope connecting many elements in each of the other panels, which feature a more unified human body, is broken and slack in *Fall*. One could connect many of the elements in *Fall* to the crucifixion site called Golgotha (the skull) and to the pouring out of the blood of Christ as artists have often placed a cup in proximity to the wounds.[40] Given Johns's use of irony throughout his other works, a Christological interpretation of the iconographic elements in the painting may not be appropriate. However, one does see the continuity between the epistemological concerns of such a recent work and his earlier works. Dichotomous thinking, which splits mind from body and splits subject from object, disrupts meaning.

Disruption of meaning is stressed if one views the four panels of *Seasons* ordered from *Spring* to *Winter* as Johns arranged them for exhibitions in 1987 and 1988. A different

31. Jasper Johns, *Fall*, 1986. Encaustic on canvas. 75 × 50 inches. Signed
UL: J.J. '86 (stenciled). Collection of the Artist. Photograph © Dorothy
Zeidman. Courtesy Jasper Johns, LC #304. © Jasper Johns/VAGA, New
York 1991.

ordering of the works emphasizes the restoration of meaningful continuity as revealed by his drawing *The Seasons* (1989: Collection of the Artist) (fig. 32). In this drawing, *Summer* comes first with its complete single human figure. (This arrangement may be Johns's original conception for the series as he painted *Summer* in 1985 and the other panels in 1986.) Then comes *Fall* with the split human body; followed by *Winter* with a reunited single human form. The concluding image is *Spring* with the older human figure standing above the child in a position akin to giving birth. Nan Rosenthal and Ruth Fine noted this changed order in that drawing as Johns

> began his left to right order of the seasons with summer, with the result that the work might be said to have an upbeat ending, concluding as it does with youth. It is a typical instance of Johns's changing variables in a drawing so that a different reading is proposed.[41]

The shared vision of Johns, Polanyi, and Wittgenstein rejects *both* the "cult of objectivity," which pretends that one may know things as they are in themselves, *and* the "cult of subjectivity," which maintains that one may only know what one projects. They mutually affirm that what is real and what can be known are functions of one's connections and interactions with the social and physical worlds in which one finds oneself. One lives on the boundary between objectivity and subjectivity. One knows one's view is limited and influenced by one's own makeup. Yet one's very awareness of these limitations constitutes a transcendence of them. On such boundaries as these, spies are more

32. Jasper Johns, *The Seasons*, 1989. Ink on plastic. 26 × 58 inches. Signed UR: J. Johns, Jan. 1989, St. Martin, F.W.I. Collection of the Artist. Photograph © Dorothy Zeidman. Courtesy of Jasper Johns, LC #D270. © Jasper Johns/VAGA, New York 1991.

useful than mere watchmen. A postmodern art suggests shapes of a postmodern theology in which each person is seen as a mind-body-in-the-world indwelling cultures and histories with others. When we are aware of our places and times, we may see more than our "dim past reversed." Then time "lifts a focus, resurrects a periscope to glimpse what joys or pain our eyes can share or answer."

4

Christo's *The Running Fence*:
Wider Communities
and the Earth

A resonance between the human body and landscape is provoked by the undulating bodies of George Segal's *The Holocaust*. The incomplete clay bodies in Stephen De Staebler's sculptures envision a connection between the human body and the earth. Land artists and process artists such as Christo take additional steps to help one sense connections to the earth. Artists increasingly create their works in settings outside museums; so, one is required to make a pilgrimage to see the art. In that pilgrimage to see the works as well as in the process to create them, one becomes aware of the communities which sustain one but which one often takes for granted. A stronger recognition of community comes into being. In such pilgrimage, one becomes aware of one's limitations, needs for others, and connections to the earth.

Art historian Joshua Taylor developed a method for discerning theological perceptions through visual art forms. This method illumines the theological import of art forms especially where there is no religious subject matter; so, his method is particularly helpful in seeing the theological significance of process and land art.

Taylor delineated how visual forms express theology.[1] He defined as "will to fellowship" or "communitive" those art forms which make the viewer sensitive to individual persons and relations. Figurative or not in subject matter, the work's style, such as Vincent van Gogh's expressionism in *La Mousmé* (1888: National Gallery of Art, Washington; Chester Dale Collection) (fig. 33), makes one aware that a person with a body painted this image. One becomes aware of oneself as a distinct bodily individual who may relate with others but never totally become completely unified with them. In contrast, Taylor identified as "will to form" and "unitive" those art forms, such as Mondrian's abstraction *Diamond Painting in Red, Yellow, and Blue* (c. 1921/1925: National Gallery of Art, Washington; Gift of Herbert and Nanette Rothschild) (fig. 34), which make one oblivious to persons as one is drawn beyond into perfect unity. Both "unitive" and "communitve" art forms are religious; but they correspond to different understandings of religion. "Unitive" corresponds to Eastern religious concern for unity with eternal ideas and absorption into oneness. "Communitive" suggests Western religious concern for community and resurrection of the body, with each individual persisting as a distinct part in the world.

Taylor's examples of the unitive ranged from Mondrian's *Diamond Painting in Red, Yellow, and Blue* to Hiram Powers's sculptures such as *Eve Tempted* (1842: National Museum of American Art, Washington, D.C.) (fig. 35), William Blake's *The Morning Stars* (from *Job*), Wassily Kandinsky's *Fuge*, Barnett Newman's *Vir Heroicus Sublimis*, and Josef Albers's *Homage to the Square*. In these works, there is a sense of completion and definition that removes one through such precise forms to a sense of order beyond that normally seen.

33. Vincent van Gogh, *La Mousmé*, 1888. Oil on canvas. 28⅞ × 23¾ inches. National Gallery of Art, Washington, Chester Dale Collection (1963.10.151 (1815)).

35. Hiram Powers, *Eve Tempted*, 1842. Marble. 68⅞ × 29⅞ × 20½ inches. National Museum of American Art, Smithsonian Institution, Washington, D.C. Museum Purchase in memory of Ralph Cross Johnson. #1968.155.126.

34. ABOVE: Piet Mondrian,
*Diamond Painting in Red,
Yellow, and Blue*, c.1921–
1925. Canvas on
fiberboard. Diagonal:
56¼ × 56 inches. National
Gallery of Art, Washington,
Gift of Herbert and
Nanette Rothschild, 1971
(2563). © Piet Mondrian/
VAGA, New York 1991.

36. RIGHT: Jean-François
Millet, *The Sower*, 19th
century. Oil on canvas.
40 × 32½ inches. Museum
of Fine Arts, Boston. Gift of
Quincy Adams Shaw
through Quincy A. Shaw,
Jr., and Mrs. Marian Shaw
Haughton (#17.1485). ©
1991 Museum of Fine Arts,
Boston. All Rights
Reserved.

> [These works] allow you to be in harmonious
> spheres, to join in . . . with a larger order without
> describing it. With a power of transport, such
> works seem to come from nature; but the artist
> uses the senses as only the means to spiritual
> unification by the discovery of perfect designs.[2]

The very precision of the works removes them from visual
reality in this will to form.

Taylor's examples of the communitive forms ranged from
Vincent Van Gogh's *La Mousmé* to Jean François Millet's
Sower (1850: Museum of Fine Arts, Boston) (fig. 36), Erich
Heckel's *Zwei Menschen in Freien*, Emil Nolde's *Last Supper* (1909: Royal Museum of Fine Arts, Copenhagen), and
Willem de Kooning's *Woman, Sag Harbor* (1964: Joseph H.
Hirshhorn Museum and Sculpture Garden, Washington,
D.C.). These works "never allow you to separate yourself
from others and human kind—never allow us to forget we
are members of a physical race."[3] There is a refusal to
organize a unity eliminating reference to selves; looking at
these works, one "never forgets that they are hand painted
. . . that an artist expressed himself" in this will to fellowship.[4]

Taylor noted that neither the unitive nor the communitive is more spiritual than the other; but they lead to
different results.

> Both are religious and concerned for religious
> values. But the religious values are not simply
> differently described means to the same end.
> They are two different means serving two different religiously described ends.[5]

In response to Taylor's analysis, theologian Theodore Gill correlated Taylor's distinctions between unitive and communitive forms in art to Emil Brunner's distinctions between Eastern and Western religions.

> Emil Brunner used to describe this distinction in the history of religions and theology as the distinction between those who reach for union and those who look for communion: those who look for some melding of the spirit with some enveloping whole as over against those who want always to maintain identity in the presence of and in the vibrant confrontation with other integrities. The unitive, he always thought, were eastern religionists; and we protestants were communionists. Another way to describe the same thing is the difference between immortality of the soul and resurrection of the body—with the immortality of the soul and its adherents not necessarily looking to a merging (but the whole teaching tilts toward everyone finally being sucked into a mush of divinity and losing detail and outline). . . . Dr. Brunner remarked that his favorite painting was in the Vatican and was the Creation of Michelangelo. God isn't touching Adam: that's the separate, the persistent idea.[6]

As Western artists become influenced by Eastern religions, there is a corresponding shift from communitive to unitive art forms, although such shifts may originate in the artist's own odyssey. Mark Rothko's paintings reflect this shift. Many of his works of the 1950s and 1960s, such as

Number 207 (Red over Dark Blue over Dark Gray), (1961: University Art Museum, Berkeley), present two sensuous pulsating abtract fields of color which prevent an experience of a unitive sensibility as the viewer is engaged first by one color field and then by the other. He called the subject matter of such works "tragedy" in part because one cannot long maintain a sustained relation with either one of the color fields.

In most of his canvases for the Rothko Chapel (1970: Houston), he eliminated such finite and communitive sensibility. One may experience the unitive senibility in most of those wall-sized works in very dark shades of purple and brown that initially seem black. The exceptions are two panels: the center panel in the front triptych and the back panel. In that front panel, the strong purples establish a more communitive sensibility as do the two fields of color in the back panel.[7]

While one may view the communitive forms as tragic because they prevent one from experiencing the unitive, the negation of the unitive experience is often associated with God's activity in Western religions. Realizing oneself to be a finite creature with limited capabilities is a corollary of acknowledging God to be Creator, and Christ to be Judge and Redeemer.[8]

Taylor's categories might mislead one into associating mystical experience exclusively with the unitive and not with the communitive, which would then be viewed instead as the realm of social concern. However, Taylor clarified that there may be mystical experience with either form, but these would be two different types of mystical experience. Examples of the communitive mystical experience in which there is not total fusion with the one are found in Martin Buber's *I and Thou* and Vladimir Lossky's *The Mystical Theology of the Eastern Church.*[9]

Taylor's correlations are an advance over those of Paul Tillich. In his early correlations of visual art and religion, Tillich saw the religious only in the expressive forms which Taylor later identified as "communitive"; while Tillich called the unitive forms dangerously irreligious.[10] Even once he had begun to appreciate Eastern religions, if not southern European Christianity, Tillich had a marked preference for those expressive forms which were dominant in his northern German homeland, and in the museums he knew in both Berlin and New York City.[11] Expressive rough-edged forms seen in Protestant theology and in northern European art span the Celtic such as the *Book of Kells*, through Mathias Grünewald such as the *Crucifixion* from the *Isenheim Altarpiece* (fig. 37) which Tillich favored so highly, to twentieth-century German expressionism, such as Erich Heckel's paintings. Perfected forms, prevalent in Roman Catholic theology and in southern European art, ranged from the ancient Greco-Roman sculpture, for example, *Aphrodite of Kyrene* (Terme Museum, Rome) (fig. 38), through the Italian Renaissance with Raphael's paintings, to certain twentieth-century abstraction.[12] This variety of communitive and unitive art within Western Christianity argues for a closer examination within Eastern religions as well, and not for an exclusive identification of the unitive with the East and the communitive with the West, even if these are characteristic emphases.

Furthermore, Taylor's discussion of the communitive is an advance over Tillich's comments which sounded as if suffering and pain were necessary ingredients in identifying a work as religious;[13] for Taylor, communitive forms are

37. Detail of the "Crucified Christ" from Mathias Grünewald, *The Isenheim Altarpiece*, 1515. Oil on wood panel. c. 12¼ × 17¾ feet overall with wings. Musée d'Unterlinden, Colmar. Courtesy Marburg/Art Resource, New York.

38. *Aphrodite of Kyrene*. Marble. Terme Museum, Rome. Courtesy Alinari/Art Resource, New York.

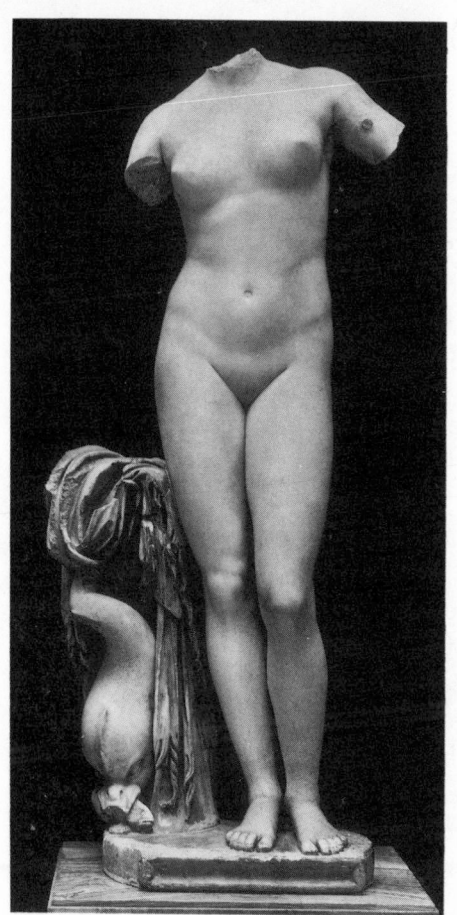

39. Detail of "Christ in Judgement" from Michelangelo, *Last Judgment*, 1541. Fresco. 48 ×44 feet overall. Sistine Chapel, Vatican City. Courtesy Alinari/Art Resource, New York.

40. Barnett Newman, *Broken Obelisk*, 1963-7. Cor-ten steel. 26 × 10½ × 10½ feet. The Rothko Chapel, Houston. Photograph by Balthazar Korab. Courtesy The Rothko Chapel.

related to finitude and are not necessarily painful. If one desires the unitive experience of the infinite, then communitive forms could be perceived as disruptive, tragic, and even painful. If one desires, however, the communitive experience, then many problematic forms could be perceived as affirmations of one's humanity to enjoy and not to escape. For instance, in many of van Gogh's works, there is a tactile quality in the expressiveness of rough lines that makes viewers aware of their own bodies; but there is nothing necessarily painful about that awareness.

A viewer's experiences, attitudes, and expectations affect what is seen or experienced in any artwork. There will be differences in evaluating works as unitive or communitive. Taylor acknowledged part of this problem: "The response to art as religious experience is as profound and as religious as the understanding of the person who looks at it makes it."[14] Our expectations govern what we see in a work. For example, if we were to visit the Tate Gallery in London and I were to say that we were about to see Jasper Johns's painting entitled Number Eight, we would probably see the number eight in the work. If I were to title it Number Three, we would see the number three. In fact the title of the work is *0 THROUGH 9* (1961: The Tate Gallery, London) and includes all the numbers superimposed on each other. Similarly, one may see condemnation in the arm and hand positions of the central Christ figure in Michelangelo's *The Last Judgment* (1535–41: Sistine Chapel, Vatican City) (fig. 39). Leo Steinberg interprets this figure in a different way by noting that the hands are in the liturgical positions for consecration and benediction of the mass from Michelangelo's period. The fresco was originally titled *The Resurrection*.[15]

As expectations vary from day to day, the same person

may experience and evaluate an artwork differently at different times. In contrast to Taylor's classification of Joseph Albers's squares as unitive, Harold Rosenberg noted that Albers considered them to be "a vibrant struggle between tones of color."[16] Rosenberg described his own changing experience of Albers's works.

> I looked around the room of fourteen paintings and three of them look as though they are ready to start a fight; and the other eleven are just sitting there square on square. And then if I come around two days later, they may all be sitting there; and none of them are jumping up and making any noise at all. And one other time, three other paintings may be hot. . . . Good thinking in modern art is that you can't always get it.[17]

In Albers's works, the lines and shapes evoke a unitive sense while the conflicting colors evoke a communitive sense. Through colors that eventually burn out our visual perception of them, a work becomes communitive by revealing our perceptual limitations.

Time spent looking at a work may reveal it as communitive when it originally looked unitive. Some of Barnett Newman's works are immediately sensed as communitive, for the rough edged black zips which run down the vertical canvases prevent any unitive experience, as in his *First Station* in *Stations of the Cross* (fig. 19). In other Newman works, however, the zip down the canvas appears to be straight-edged and admits a unitive experience; that is, until one has looked at the line a long time and discovered a subtle curve or roughness at the bottom of the zip, a feature that disrupts the unitive relation with the work. Yet other works by Newman, such as the eighteen-foot-wide *Vir Heroicus Sublimis* (1950–51: The Museum of Modern Art, New York) are classified by Taylor as unitive. Even after an extended viewing of that large red painting with its small hard-edged vertical zips, the unitive experience is maintained. An artist may do both unitive and communitive works. So, each art work must be carefully examined to sense its effects before it is correlated with theological ideas.

The difference between communitive and unitive is clarified by Barnett Newman's *Broken Obelisk* (1963–67; Rothko Chapel, Houston) (fig. 40), which is communitive as the top of the work appears broken or shattered. If the broken section were cut off so that the top were to appear level, then the work would become closer to unitive sensibility. As a communitive work, it was appropriately dedicated to the memory of Martin Luther King.[18] With Taylor's method, one may perceive spiritual dimensions in art works without overt religious subject matter.

Robert Smithson's *Spiral Jetty* (1970: Rozel Point, The Great Salt Lake, Utah) is one of the best known examples of twentieth-century land art. While the work is now below the rising lake's surface, one could originally walk on top of the jetty which was designed so that viewers would realize their own bodily natures. Such realization increases awareness of connection to the rest of the earth. Walking to the site made one aware of one's own body; and so, the artwork is "communitive" in Taylor's categories. Walking on the *Spiral Jetty* (with its irregular changing, unpredictable surface extending fifteen hundred feet long and fifteen feet wide) made one aware of changing combinations of one's own musculature. In a manner similar to the changes in

Jasper Johns's works, the changes in *Spiral Jetty* also required one to pay attention. John Coplans describes some of these dynamics:

> In the *Spiral Jetty*, I think one of Smithson's interests lay in the stumbling aspect of walking, forcing one to pay attention to where one is going. I'm told that when he finished the *Spiral Jetty*, Smithson ripped up the boulders so that the pathway couldn't be negotiated smoothly.
>
> Evidently Smithson wanted to make the locomotion discontinous—to disrupt it. . . . You become unusually aware of the physicality of your body in relationship to its surroundings, of temperature, of the movement of the wind, of the sounds of nature, and of how isolated you have been from nature until this moment.[19]

As Coplan notes, Smithson was "fully aware of The Fall,"[20] and others have spoken of Smithson's religious insights.[21] His vision of the earth was complex, recognizing destructive and constructive impulses. Smithson noted, "The certainty of the absolute garden would never be regained."[22] His art does not attempt to regenerate wastelands as some others's land art does;[23] but he gives us a vision of the complexities involved in working with a fallen creation.

Walter De Maria's *Lightning Field* (1977), opened to the public in 1978, is another example of a communicative art work. To reach the site, one must drive four hours from Albuquerque, New Mexico. The sense of pilgrimage is heightened by an almost monastic lifestyle at the site: committing oneself to several days with others, viewing the work at different hours, eating in common, and spending extended time in silence.

Hundreds of highly polished steel poles (from fifteen feet to over twenty-nine feet in height) are placed 220 feet apart, extending one mile along an east-west axis and one kilometer along a north-south axis. The land is uneven; but the different heights of the poles allow for an even alignment of their tops. Melinda Wortz describes the effect of standing in the *Lightning Field* which gives the viewer a sense of place connecting one to creation and a center beyond oneself:

> The straight lines articulated by the lightning poles here exist in vertical as well as horizontal space, and more particularly . . . orient our awareness to the spaces . . . above and below and between them, the organic spaces of nature. Thus the *Lightning Field* presents a meeting of intellectual order and random rhythm, of structure and chaos, of logic and invention, of man and nature. It is important to see that this meeting is not intended to express the domination or control of nature by man but rather just the opposite. As described, De Maria's grid acts to make us aware of our place in the universe, infinitesimal but integral.[24]

Melinda Wortz details also how this work moves us beyond subject/object dichotomies. Towering over the viewer, any two poles make the viewer aware of the space between the two more than one normally is when looking ahead or focusing on particulars in one's environment. One usually perceives oneself and objects in the environment as separate from each other and the surrounding space; but standing below the poles, with their surfaces reflecting the colors of the ground, the light of the sky, and oneself, one perceives the poles connecting earth and sky. "As human beings we have the same vertical orientation as the poles. We too are bridges between the earth and sky—how often do we perceive ourselves in this manner?"[25]

The *Lightning Field* cultivates awareness of connections to a center beyond oneself as experienced through George Segal's *The Holocaust* or Orthodox icons. Many of the artworks considered in this book give one a sense of place and time. Yet there are important differences between the infinitesimal place given the viewer by *Lightning Field* and the modest but personal space given by Segal's *The Holocaust*, the icons, or De Staebler's sculptures. Christo's *The Running Fence* came closer than De Maria's *Lightning Field* in affirming such personal space.

A major work of process art, *The Running Fence, Sonoma and Marin Counties, California 1972–76* (fig. 41) was created by New York-based artist Christo (b. 1935). Stretched 24½ miles across Marin and Sonoma counties in northern California for two weeks in September 1976, the artwork was made of white nylon, eighteen feet high, suspended by steel cables. The work began east of Highway 101 and ran west (fig. 42) until dipping into the Pacific Ocean (fig. 43). One encounters it first not at the beginning but at some point along the way, just as one encounters so many life situations already created and making one aware of oneself as a creature. As hills obscured one's vision, one could not see some portions of the fence. The resulting sense of incompletion is analogous to that sensed in De Staebler's sculptures.

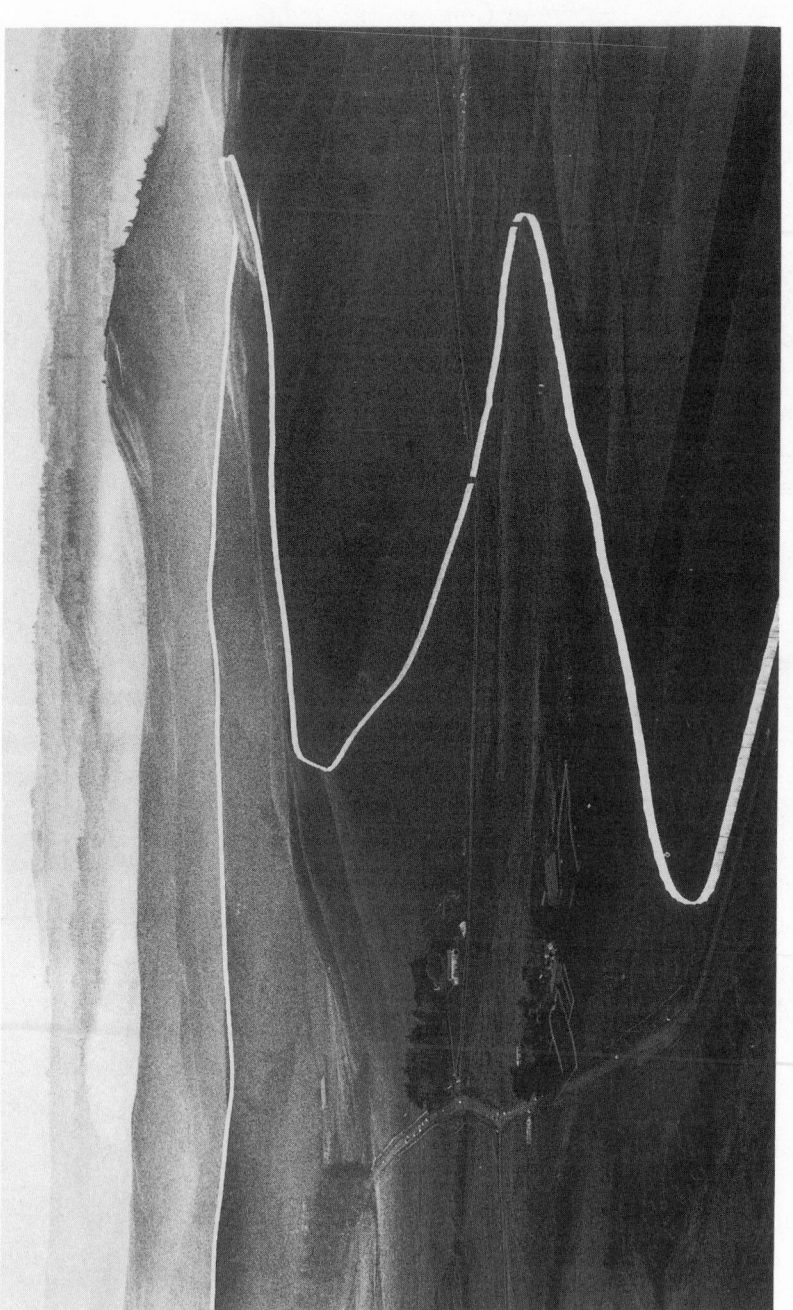

41. Christo, *The Running Fence, Sonoma and Marin Counties, Ca., 1972-6.* 18 feet high, 24½ miles long. Photograph by Gianfranco Gorgoni. Courtesy Christo. © Christo 1976.

The fence drew the viewer into relationships with the landscape as it called attention to the shapes of the hills and the colors of its surroundings, including some wooden white fences along the way. At times, *The Running Fence* reflected the blues of the sky or the browns of the earth. At sunrise or sunset, pink and purple filled the fence. Every movement of the wind was made visible by the fence. It often appeared as a ribbon of light moving across the hills, linking all aspects of the landscape and leading one beyond what one could see (fig. 44).

The theological importance of the work may be understood through the experiences of transcendence it afforded the viewers and the creators. The work was sublime as it led the viewers to sense interrelationships with the features of nature beyond them; while some of those features remained hidden and mysterious. The viewer's finitude was stressed by the 24½ mile size; for the whole work could not be seen from any one place. Part of it could not be seen at all; for it was on land beyond fences.

In many previous artworks, Christo has emphasized human finitude and the mystery of creation by wrapping structures. When a building or a coast line or a wall is wrapped in fabric, one knows there is more than one can see. As one could not see all of *The Running Fence* because it disappeared behind hills where one was not permitted to go, so also one could not see all the art museum in *Wrapped Kunsthalle, Bern, Switzerland 1968* (fig. 45) or the rocky coast in *Wrapped Coast, Little Bay, Australia, 1969* (fig. 46) or the wall in *The Wall—Wrapped Roman Wall, Rome 1974* (fig. 48).

In that wrapping process, art historian Dominique Laporte discerned explicit connections with the Christian tradition through what she called "the shroud syndrome or

42. Detail of Christo, *The Running Fence*. Photograph by Wolfgang Volz. Courtesy Christo. © Christo 1976.

43. Detail of Christo, *The Running Fence*. Photograph by Wolfgang Volz. Courtesy Christo. © Christo 1976.

44. Detail of Christo, *The Running Fence*. Photograph by Wolfgang Volz. Courtesy Christo. © Christo 1976.

the phantasm of resurrection."[26] Noting that Christo dropped his last name (Javacheff) and abbreviated his given name into a new surname, she asserted, "Christo's name is the very essence of his work."[27] Wrapped for only a few days, the structures may remind one of Christ's time in the tomb. The unveiling then reminds one of the moment of resurrection.[28]

When a structure is wrapped, it appears to be a present at a party. One may then look at human structures as well as natural environments as gifts. Helping the viewer see creation as a gift is a religious ingredient in Christo's work and resonates with Taylor's communitive category where the viewer becomes conscious that an artwork was made by another body. When one sees something wrapped, one may think of the other who took the time and effort to wrap it; for wrapping involves intentional time and physical effort.

Required to drive and periodically to walk on a day-long trip to view much of the fence, viewers became more conscious of their own bodies. Becoming aware of their own finitude is a major step toward becoming aware of God. As they realize that they are creatures dependent upon what is beyond their control, then they may become aware of the Creator who shapes and sustains them.

In a museum, one may be able to pretend that one is in control and can see everything; but trying to see *The Running Fence* made one aware how limited one is. Since the fence ran across dozens of jurisdictions including fifty-nine privately owned ranches, the viewer became aware of the different political entities (with their different policies for approaching the fence). One became acquainted also with a number of ranchers, some of whom did not allow one to

45. Christo, *Wrapped Kunsthalle, Bern, Switzerland*, 1968. 27,000 square feet of synthetic fabric and 10,000 feet of rope. Photograph by Thomas Cugini. Courtesy Christo. © Christo 1968.

46. Christo, *Wrapped Coast, Little Bay, Australia,* 1969. One million square feet. Coordinator John Kaldon. Photograph by Harry Shunk. Courtesy Christo. © Christo 1969.

48. Christo, *The Wall—Wrapped Roman Wall, Rome, Via Vittorio Veneto and Villa Borghese,* 1974. Woven synthetic fabric and rope. Height: 55 feet. Length: 1,100 feet. Photograph by Harry Shunk. Courtesy Christo. © Christo 1974.

cross their land to view the fence as it ran down a gully or behind a barn. Another dimension of one's finitude was made evident when one was surprised as the artwork appeared from behind a hill or out of a previously unnoticed valley. When one is surprised, one realizes that one is not all knowing.

Building the artwork revealed the interrelations of many distinct communities. In process art, seeing these interrelations is part of the art experience. As they tried to support or oppose the fence's construction, many persons realized for the first time not only the different political jurisdictions in which they lived but also the different views held by their neighbors. The litigation over the fence made evident the profiles of different persons and groups in the communities. The several years of planning revealed individual characteristics of different ranchers and political jurisdictions as different settlements were made with each of them. For instance, breaks in the fence were designed to accommodate the primary travel routes in each ranch or political jurisdiction. This accommodation required each rancher and community to realize explicitly which ways they traveled regularly, something they had only tacitly known.

Christo's most recent proposal, *The Umbrellas*, would lead one to see one's connection across even wider distances than the 24½ miles of *The Running Fence*. At a time when some United States politicians would create trade barriers to obscure relations with countries of Asia, Christo would lift thousands of umbrellas in both California and Japan to help all see "the similarities and differences in the ways of life in two valleys,"[29] one seventy miles north of Tokyo and the other sixty miles north of Los Angeles. In the 1990s, Christo's *The Umbrellas* will help one see even wider possibilities for fellowship with others of this earth who are otherwise separated by its widest ocean.

Christo has chosen sites which present seemingly impossible bureaucratic or legal barriers. To run a fence 24½ miles across dozens of different jurisidictions raises political problems which could have been avoided by building the fence on one ranch or within one county. Showing that freedom to create is possible even in the most unlikely places is an important agenda for Christo, who grew up first under Nazi and later Soviet occupation. Christo said, "Freedom is most important to me and my work."[30] The 24½ mile length of *Running Fence* parodied the twenty-four kilometer length of the Berlin wall; and his wife Jeanne Claude Christo noted the delight Christo took in that extra half mile.[31] The half mile introduced irregularity and seemed to tweak the noses of those who build walls and regulations to require conformity in life and rounded-off figures in government forms. Christo provided a prophetic statement about the Berlin wall and the iron curtain in his *Valley Curtain, Grand Hogback, Rifle, Colorado, 1970–72* (fig. 47); for in that windy valley, the curtain was quickly ripped to pieces. His projects stress that walls, curtains, and fences may not last for long; as an example, *Running Fence* was scheduled to come down after only two weeks. His works communicate one's finitude in time as well as space.[32]

Remembering George Segal's preferences for daily space and Jasper Johns's ways of overcoming object/subject dichotomies, one may sense their affinities with Christo's concerns as he describes art in these terms.

I think all the power and force of art comes from

real life, that the work must be so much a part of
everyday life that it cannot be separated.[33]

Using Joshua Taylor's terms, this work can be identified
as spiritually "communitive." The artwork occasioned the
awareness of one's own body and finitude as well as the
recognition of other distinct individuals and groups. The
Running Fence did more than make one aware of the distinct personalities of one's communities; for it also brought
together individuals who would otherwise have remained
unknown to each other. Even after the fence has been down
for many years, one cannot walk or drive along that stretch
of northern California without remembering the wider possibilities for fellowship which *The Running Fence* revealed.

When postmodern theologies are written, one may expect them to include some of these possibilities for fellowship as well as other connections noted in earlier
chapters. With George Segal's art, one moves beyond a
sense of loss still evident in Mark Taylor's postmodern a/
theology and toward a sense of place connected to biblical
subject matter and a center beyond oneself. In Stephen De
Staebler's art, there is a recovery of relation with religious
forms and times of graceful aging, dying, and rising as well
as a recovery of commitment to dinner table conversation in
contrast to cocktail party chatter. Through Jasper Johns's
art, one perceives postcritical philosophies beyond subject/
object and mind/body dichotomies. The reaffirmations of
one's own body in art and philosophy extend to an appreciation of one's relationships with wider communities and the
earth as evidenced by Christo's process art and others's land
art which invite pilgrimage to see the world as a gift.

Human bodies generate a sense of relation. These artistic

47. Christo, *Valley Curtain, Grand Hogback, Rifle, Colorado*, 1971-2.
Span: 1250 feet. Height: 185-365 feet. 200,000 square feet of nylon
polyamide. 110,000 pounds of steel cables. Project Director: Jan van der
Marck. Photograph by Harry Shunk. Courtesy Christo. © Christo 1972.

works not only communicate a sense of wholeness to which
the body parts relate (in contrast to modern art's fragmented parts) but also generate family groupings reminding us of relations with others beyond ourselves and our
time. Many of Segal's early works featured an isolated individual in lonely surroundings; but his recent works (including the *Holocaust* and *Abraham's Farewell to Ishmael*)
provide perceptions of family relations and biblical traditions which transcend seeming brokenness. The bodies in
Segal's works also remind us of our connections to the
earth. Each of De Staebler's earlier works featured a fragmented or emerging body communicating an affirmation of
the incomplete individual and his or her relation with the
earth. De Staebler's recent *Pietà* introduces relationship
between two figures who merge in ways establishing a
sense of place and time missing in much modern thought.
Johns's art has similarly developed from earlier body fragments and isolated individuals into the full human figure
and its progeny as in his most recent drawing of *Seasons*.
Christo's work evokes awareness not only of death and
resurrection but also of our own bodies and their complex
relations to many communities and the earth. These artists
help us perceive not only connections but also transcendent relations which lead us to center beyond ourselves and
to sense not only our time and our place but also other
generations and the earth beyond our place and our time.

Notes

Chapter 1: George Segal's *The Holocaust*

1. Sam Hunter and Don Hawthorne, *George Segal* (New York: Rizzoli, 1984), 14. Residual references to the human form in Barnett Newman's work (verticality and human size of the canvas) are noted by Jane Dillenberger, *"The Stations of the Cross* by Barnett Newman," in her *Secular Art with Sacred Theme* (Nashville: Abingdon Press, 1969), and by Lawrence Alloway, "Residual Sign Systems in Abstract Expressionism," *Artforum* 12 (1973): 36–42.

2. George Segal, interview by Doug Adams, 20 February, 1988 (hereafter, Segal Interview).

3. Ibid.

4. Jo Milgrom, *The Binding of Isaac: The Akedah—A Primary Symbol in Jewish Thought and Art* (Berkeley: BIBAL Press, 1988), 280.

5. Ibid.

6. Jane Dillenberger, "George Segal's *Abraham and Isaac*: Some Iconographic Reflections," in *Art, Creativity, and the Sacred*, ed. Diane Apostolos-Cappadona (New York: Crossroad, 1984), 105–24.

7. Milgrom, *The Binding of Isaac*, 54–55.

8. Segal Interview.

9. Ibid. Those were Segal's words when I explicitly asked him about the Christological interpretation of the central figure from the perspective of the body at the central figure's right foot. That interpretation along with the other foregoing ones were in a draft I had sent to him earlier as the basis for the interview.

10. Ibid.

11. Cf. Søren Kierkegaard, *Fear and Trembling* and *Repetition*, ed. and trans. Howard V. Hong and Edna H. Hong (Princeton: Princeton University Press, 1983), 9–23.

12. Michael Brenson, "Why Segal Is Doing Holocaust Memorial," *New York Times*, 8, April 1983, p. C16.

13. Cf. Doug Adams, "Informing Religious Studies With Contemporary and Earlier Visual Arts Portraying the Human Body: A Kinesthetic Teaching Method," in *Art As Religious Studies*, ed. Doug Adams and Diane Apostolos-Cappadona (New York: Crossroad, 1987), 196.

14. Hunter and Hawthorne, *George Segal*, 122.

15. Segal Interview.

16. Ibid.

17. Diane Apostolos-Cappadona, "Martha Graham and the Quest for The Feminine in Eve, Lilith, and Judith," in *Dance As Religious Studies*, ed. Doug Adams and Diane Apostolos-Cappadona (New York: Crossroad, l990), chapter 9, passim.

18. Segal Interview.

19. Peggy Isaak Gluck, "Controversy Shadows Dedication," *Northern California Jewish Bulletin*, 2 November 1984.

20. Segal Interview.

21. Ibid.

22. Ibid.

23. Ibid.

24. Ibid.

25. Ibid.

26. Ibid.

27. Pierre Restany to George Segal, letter dated 25 February 1985.

28. Segal Interview.

29. Ibid.

30. Ibid. In this interview, Segal confirmed these details from his earlier conversation with the Dillenbergers.

31. Andrea Liss, *J.A.C.O.B.S. Letter*, January-March 1984, no pagination.

32. Comparisons could be made between Wiesel's treatment

of the Holocaust in his novels and Segal's treatment of the Holocaust in art. Such comparisons would consider their critics as well as the artists' inclusions of Christ-imagery.

33. John Felstiner, *J.A.C.O.B.S. Letter*, April-June 1984, p. 19.

34. Allen Temko, "The Virtues and Flaws of the Segal Sculpture," *San Francisco Chronicle*, 8 November 1984, sec. A, p. 2.

35. Ira Kamin, "Holocaust Monument Speaks of Man's Inhumanity," *Northern California Jewish Bulletin*, 16 November 1984, pp. 3f.

36. Edward Rodati, *J.A.C.O.B.S. Letter*, April-June 1984, no pagination.

37. Brenson, "Why Segal Is Doing Holocaust Memorial," p. C16.

38. David Wright, *The Berkeley Voice*, 19 December 1984, p. 14.

39. "Segal's Holocaust Memorial," *Art In America*, Summer 1983, p. 136.

40. Victor Frankl, *From Death-Camp to Existentialism: A Psychiatrist's Path to a New Therapy*, trans. Ilse Lasch (Boston: Beacon Press, 1959).

41. Alice Lok Cahana, interview by Doug Adams, 10 April 1988 (hereafter, Cahana Interview).

42. Barbara Rose, "From Ashes to the Rainbow," in *From Ashes to the Rainbow: A Tribute to Raoul Wallenberg, Works by Alice Lok Cahana* (Los Angeles: Hebrew Union College, Skirball Museum, 1986), 18.

43. Cahana Interview.

44. Rose, "From Ashes to the Rainbow," in *From Ashes to the Rainbow*, p. 34.

45. Michael Brenson, "George Segal, 'The Holocaust,'" *New York Times*, 30 August 1985, p. C26.

46. Beth Coffelt, quoted in *Northern California Jewish Bulletin*, 2 November 1984, no pagination.

47. Mark Taylor, *Erring: A Postmodern A/Theology* (Chicago: University of Chicago Press, 1984), 6.

48. Charles Jencks, *Post-Modernism: The New Classicism in*

Art and Architecture (New York: Rizzoli, 1987), 350.

49. Ibid., 11.

Chapter 2: Stephen De Staebler's Sculptures

1. Leonid Ouspensky, *Theology of the Icon* (Crestwood, NY: St. Vladimir's Seminary Press, 1978), 224–27.

2. Robert Byron and David Talbot Rice, *The Birth of Western Painting* (New York: Hacker Art Book, 1968).

3. Militsia Zernov, "The Icon of the Holy Trinity of Rublev," *Sobornost*, Winter 1972, pp. 387–94.

4. Margaret R. Miles, *Image as Insight: Visual Understanding in Western Christianity and Secular Culture* (Boston: Beacon Press, 1985), 32.

5. Joseph P. Frary, "The Logic of Icons," *Sobornost*, Winter 1972, p. 403.

6. Byron and Rice, *The Birth of Western Painting*, passim.

7. Stephen De Staebler and Diane Apostolos-Cappadona, "Reflections on Art and the Spirit: A Conversation" in *Art, Creativity, and the Sacred*, ed. Diane Apostolos-Cappadona (New York: Crossroad, 1984), 24–33.

8. Donald Kuspit, *Stephen De Staebler: The Figure* (San Francisco: Chronicle Book, 1988), 15.

9. Stephen De Staebler, interview by Doug Adams, 25 March 1987 (hereafter, De Staebler Interview 1).

10. De Staebler and Apostolos-Cappadona, "Reflections on Art and the Spirit," 29.

11. Ted Lindberg, *Stephen De Staebler: An Exhibition of Recent Bronzes* (Vancouver: Emily Carr College of Art and the Art Museum Association of America, 1983), 8.

12. De Staebler Interview 1.

13. Ibid.

14. Ibid.

15. Ibid.

16. Ibid.

17. Ibid.

18. Doug Adams and Diane Apostolos-Cappadona, "Art As

Religious Studies: Insights Into the Judeo-Christian Traditions"
in *Art As Religious Studies*, ed. Doug Adams and Diane Apostolos-Cappadona (New York: Crossroad, 1987), 8.

19. De Staebler Interview 1.

20. Many art works of the 1950s featuring the incomplete
human form were similar to Baskin's in decrying flaws in the
world. Cf. Peter Selz, *New Images of Man* (New York: The
Museum of Modern Art, 1959).

21. De Staebler Interview 1.

22. In New Harmony, Jane Blaffer Owen has encouraged the
concentration of fine architecture and art including Philip
Johnson's Roofless Church (1960: New Harmony) with one of the
three castings of Jacques Lipchitz's *Descent of the Spirit*; Richard
Meier's *Visitor Center* and *Pottery Studio*; and Paul Tillich's burial
site. The Roofless Church was originally designed without a
curving line by Philip Johnson. Jane Blaffer Owen rejected that
design and suggested a shape generated by Ted Shawn's choreog-
raphy of the Doxology which included a repeated gesture of the
hands moving together upwards in front of the body to a position
above the head and then separating and sweeping down to both
sides thus creating an oval shape circumscribing the torso. The
interior of the structure is like a large rib cage. Jane Blaffer
Owen, interview by Doug Adams, 8 May 1987.

23. De Staebler Interview 1. In a later interview, I shared my
correlation of the torso with the deepest part of the groove; De
Staebler responded, "I like your identifying the deepest central
part . . . as the torso. One of the great experiences I had after
shaping that was with the groove. You just lie back into it. Your
body can go back . . . and then you look up and then you see this
cavity as if you were in a canoe." Stephen De Staebler, interview
by Doug Adams, 3 March 1989 (hereafter, De Staebler Interview
2).

24. De Staebler Interview 1.

25. *Saint Benedict: Father of Western Civilization*, ed. Diana
de Froment and trans. Elsie Callender (Antwerp: Mercatorfonds,
1981), no pagination.

26. De Staebler Interview 1.

27. De Staebler and Apostolos-Cappadona, "Art and the Spirit," 28–9.

28. Ibid., 29.

29. Ted Lindberg, *Stephen De Staebler*, 7.

30. De Staebler Interview 2.

31. Ibid.

32. Ibid.

33. Ibid.

34. Ibid.

35. Ibid.

36. Ibid.

37. Ibid.

38. Ibid.

39. Ibid.

40. Ibid.

41. Ibid.

42. Ibid.

43. Ibid.

44. Ibid.

45. Ibid.

46. Ibid.

47. Ibid.

48. Ibid.

49. Ibid.

50. Jane Blaffer Owen, one page brochure about the De Staebler *Pietà*, New Harmony, fall 1989.

51. Thomas Albright, "Review of Exhibition," *San Francisco Chronicle*, 4 February 1977.

52. Jane Dillenberger and John Dillenberger, *Perceptions of the Spirit in Twentieth Century American Art* (Indianapolis: Indianapolis Museum of Art, 1977), 158.

Chapter 3: Jasper Johns's Paintings

1. Jill Johnston, "Tracking the Shadow," *Art in America*, October 1987, 129–42, especially n. 9 on p. 142. Johns stated that he first saw the *Isenheim Altarpiece* in 1976 and then again in 1979;

but he began tracing various images from a portfolio of Grünewald details which was given to him in 1980. Nan Rosenthal
and Ruth E. Fine, *The Drawings of Jasper Johns* (Washington,
DC: National Gallery of Art, 1990), 82.

2. Kozloff, quoted in Richard S. Field, *Jasper Johns Prints
1960–1970* (New York: Praeger, 1970), no pagination.

3. Stein, quoted in Field, *Jasper Johns Prints*.

4. Ludwig Wittgenstein, *Philosophical Investigations* (New
York: Macmillan, 1953), 109, #340.

5. Michael Polanyi, *Knowing and Being* (Chicago: University
of Chicago Press, 1969), 148.

6. Field, *Jasper Johns Prints*, no pagination.

7. Ibid.

8. Ibid.

9. Wittgenstein, *Philosophical Investigations*, 11, #23

10. Leo Steinberg, "Contemporary Art and the Plight of the
Public," *The New Art: A Critical Anthology*, ed. Gregory Battcock (New York: Dutton, 1966), 43.

11. Alan Solomon, "The New Art," in *The New Art: A Critical
Anthology*, ed. Gregory Battcock (New York: Dutton, 1966), 82.

12. Leo Steinberg, *Jasper Johns* (New York: George Witten-
born, 1963), passim.

13. Field, *Jasper Johns Prints*, no pagination.

14. John Cage, "Jasper Johns: Stories and Ideas" reprinted in
Alan Solomon, *Jasper Johns: Paintings, Drawings, and Sculpture
1954–1964* (London: Whitechapel Gallery, 1964), 27–28.

15. Solomon, *Jasper Johns*, 24.

16. Kent speaks the line to Lear who has been mislead into
thinking that Goneril and Regan love him because they say the
word love and that Cordelia does not love him because she will
not speak the word (act I, sc. 4, lines 99–100).

17. Wittgenstein, *Philosophical Investigations*, 46, #107.

18. Solomon, *Jasper Johns*, 25.

19. Michael Polanyi, *Personal Knowledge: Towards A Post-
Critical Philosophy* (Chicago: University of Chicago Press, 1958),
65.

20. Field, *Jasper Johns Prints*, no pagination.

21. Ibid.

22. Johns, quoted in G. R. Swenson, "What Is Pop Art? Part II: Jasper Johns," *Art News*, 62, no. 10 (February 1964): 66.

23. Johns, quoted in Solomon, *Jasper Johns*, 19.

24. Wittgenstein, *Philosophical Investigations*, 8, #18

25. Solomon, *Jasper Johns*, 7–8.

26. Field, *Jasper Johns Prints*, no pagination.

27. Cage in Solomon, *Jasper Johns*, 29.

28. Solomon, *Jasper Johns*, 16.

29. Joseph Young, "Jasper Johns: An Appraisal," *Art International* 13, no. 7 (September 1969): 52.

30. Barbara Rose, "Device Circle," description accompanying print, (n.p., n.d.)

31. Solomon, *Jasper Johns*, 21.

32. Polanyi, *Personal Knowledge*, x. Robert Irwin is another artist whose work parallels Polanyi's explorations of the tacit and explicit dimensions of knowing. He notes some of the ways his works are in conversation with Polanyi's thought: cf. Robert Irwin, *Being and Circumstance: Notes Toward a Conditional Art* (Larkspur Landing, CA: Lapis Press, 1985), 10–11 and 24.

33. Field, *Jasper Johns Prints*, no pagination.

34. McLuhan, quoted in Field, *Jasper Johns Prints*.

35. Ibid.

36. Jill Johnston, "Tracking the Shadow," passim.

37. Ibid.

38. Ibid.

39. Mark Rosenthal, *Jasper Johns: Work Since 1974* (Philadelphia: Philadelphia Museum of Art, 1989), 97.

40. Doug Adams, "Becoming the Body of Christ in Resurrected Communion," *Church Teachers* March/May 1989, p. 178.

41. Rosenthal and Fine, *The Drawings of Jasper Johns*, 41.

Chapter 4: Christo's *The Running Fence*

1. I have reported Joshua Taylor's interpretations in the periodical of the Society for the Arts, Religion, and Contemporary Culture: Doug Adams, "Insights From 'Three Perspectives on

the Religious and Aesthetic Imagination,'" *Seedbed* 3, no. 3 (June 1975): 1–3; and in my "Theological Expressions Through Visual Art Forms," in *Art, Creativity, and the Sacred*, ed. Diane Apostolos-Cappadona (New York: Crossroad, 1984), 311–18.

2. Ibid., 313.

3. Ibid.

4. Ibid., 313–14.

5. Ibid., 314

6. Ibid.

7. Roger Wedell, "Berdyaev and Rothko: Transformative Visions" in *Art, Creativity, and the Sacred*, 306 and 310, n. 8. The front panel would correspond to the placement of the Celestial Madonna and Child and the back panel would correspond to the placement of the Last Judgment in the Torcello Baptistry which was a favorite of Rothko when he visited Venice.

8. Edward Hobbs outlined this theological interpretation in the second lecture of the Jane and John Dillenberger Endowment for the Visual Arts, The Graduate Theological Union, Berkeley, 18 December 1981.

9. Martin Buber, *I and Thou*, trans. Walter Kaufman, (New York: Charles Scribner's Sons, 1970); and Vladimir Lossky, *The Mystical Theology of the Eastern Church*, (London: James Clarke and Co. Ltd., 1957).

10. Paul Tillich, "Existentialist Aspects of Modern Art," in *Christianity and the Existentialists*, ed. Carl Michalson (New York: Charles Scribner's Sons, 1956), 128–47; and reprinted in Paul Tillich, *On Art and Architecture* ed. John Dillenberger (New York: Crossroad, 1987), 89–101.

11. His later more sophisticated categories are evident in two other essays: "Art and Ultimate Reality," and "Religious Dimensions of Contemporary Art," in *On Art and Architecture*, 139–57 and 171–87, respectively.

12. Jane Dillenberger suggested the contrasts between these forms in the first lecture of the Jane and John Dillenberger Endowment for the Visual Arts, The Graduate Theological Union, Berkeley, 25 February 1981: "Michelangelo vs. Grünewald: A Study of Northern and Italian Sensibilities at the Time

of the Reformation." A revised version of this lecture is included in Jane Dillenberger, *Image and Spirit in Sacred and Secular Art*, ed. Diane Apostolos-Cappadona (New York: Crossroad, 1990).

13. John Dixon developed this criticism of Tillich in his article, "Is tragedy essential to knowing? A critique of Dr. Tillich's aesthetic," *Journal of Religion* 43 (October 1963): 271–84.

14. Adams, "Theological Expressions Through Visual Art Forms," 315.

15. Leo Steinberg, "Michelangelo's 'Last Judgment' as Merciful Heresy," *Art In America*, November-December 1975, 49–63. Cf. Marcia Hall, "Michelangelo's Last Judgment: Resurrection of the Body and Predestination," *Art Bulletin* 58 (March 1976): 85–92.

16. Doug Adams, "Theological Expressions Through Visual Art Forms," 315.

17. Ibid., 315–16.

18. There were three renderings of *Broken Obelisk*: the University of Washington in Seattle, the Museum of Modern Art in New York, and the Rothko Chapel in Houston.

19. John Coplans, "Robert Smithson, *The Amarillo Ramp*," in *Robert Smithson: Sculpture*, ed. Robert Hobbs (Ithaca and London: Cornell University Press, 1981), 54.

20. Ibid., 55.

21. Robert Hobbs, "Introduction," to *Robert Smithson: Sculpture*, 12; and Jane Dillenberger and John Dillenberger, *Perceptions of the Spirit in Twentieth-Century American Art*, (Indianapolis: Indianapolis Museum of Art, 1977), 33–34 and 160.

22. Robert Smithson, "A Sedimentation of the Mind: Earth Projects," *The Writings of Robert Smithson*, ed. Nancy Holt (New York: New York University Press, 1979), 91.

23. Patricia Runo, "Reclamation, Resacralization, and Regeneration: Approaches to the Environment in the Art of Smithson, Singer, and the Harrisons," *The Cry of the Environment and Rebuilding the Christian Creation Tradition*, ed. Philip Joranson and Ken Butigan (Santa Fe: Bear and Co., 1984), 270–95.

24. Melinda Wortz, "Walter De Maria's *The Lightning Field*," *Arts Magazine* 54, no. 9 (May 1980): 173.

25. Ibid.

26. Dominique G. Laporte, *Christo*, trans. Abby Pollak (New York: Pantheon Books, 1988), 67.

27. Ibid.

28. Ibid.

29. Christo, interview by Doug Adams, 16 April 1988 (hereafter, Christo Interview). Before interviewing Christo and his wife, Jeanne-Claude, who administers his C.V.J. corporation, I sent them a draft of this chapter. We had corresponded four years earlier in connection with my analysis of *The Running Fence* in "Theological Expressions Through Visual Art Forms," pp. 316–18. I interviewed Jeanne-Claude by phone on 12 April 1988 (Hereafter, J.-C. Christo Interview). We discussed how their enjoyment of the widest variety of interpretations is another way they invite the participation of all in the community: as Jeanne-Claude noted, "He is delighted to see a variety of interpretations because his work is not the usual sculpture. . . . Christo's temporary large scale works of art call for a variety of interpretations; and therefore, everything I read in your text was a joy to read" (J.-C. Christo Interview). For two days, as part of the 15 April opening of the exhibition, "Christo and Peter Selz: The Running Fence Project Revisited," at the Graduate Theological Union Library in Berkeley, their continuing care was apparent for those who worked on *The Running Fence* and who returned in large number for the exhibition. Jeanne-Claude had commented, "They become part of our family; so, of course we take good care of them." (J.-C. Christo Interview).

30. Christo Interview.

31. J.-C. Christo Interview.

32. In 1972, Christo first conceived of both *The Running Fence* and *Wrapped Reichstag, a project for Berlin*. The latter has not yet been achieved.

33. Christo Interview.